VIKINGS IN RUSSIA
Yngvar's Saga and Eymund's Saga

VIKINGS IN RUSSIA

Yngvar's Saga and Eymund's Saga

Translated and Introduced by
HERMANN PÁLSSON AND PAUL EDWARDS

EDINBURGH UNIVERSITY PRESS

© 1989
Hermann Palsson and Paul Edwards

Edinburgh University Press
22 George Square, Edinburgh

Set in Linotron Plantin
by Photoprint, Torquay, and
printed in Great Britain by
Redwood Burn Limited
Trowbridge, Wilts.

British Library Cataloguing
  in Publication Data
Vikings in Russia:
    Yngvar's saga and Eymund's saga.
I. Palsson, Hermann
II. Edwards, Paul, *1926 July 31*–
839'.68

ISBN 0 85224 623 4
ISBN 0 85224 650 1 pbk

CONTENTS

INTRODUCTION

The two Icelandic sagas in this volume open a small window on the hazy world of Scandinavian Vikings in eleventh-century Russia. The brief glimpses they give us of an obscure corner of European history are intriguing, not so much because of the light they throw on the lives of Yngvar Eymundsson and Eymund Hringsson as for the elusive quality of narrative. Although these sagas appear to contain references to actual events, they include so many purely fictive elements that it is not always possible to separate facts from the products of the authors' fertile imagination; the two elements that went into the making of the sagas, historical fact and creative story-writing, are sometimes barely perceptibly, sometimes extravagantly, fused together. In other words, we are dealing with authors whose concern for historical accuracy was not allowed to interfere with the serious business of providing suitable material for entertainment. However, even the most tenuous links with historical events are essential for the purpose of making sense of the sagas; their thirteenth-century audiences would probably enjoy these tales both for their entertainment value and for what they taught, or seemed to teach, about the world and the past.

The principal aim of this introduction is to explore the intellectual background of the two sagas. We shall attempt to indicate their relationship to each other and to medieval Icelandic saga writing as a whole. The reader will find it helpful to bear in mind that not only Russia and remoter regions were very distant from the authors and their audience, but that even Scandinavia itself lay far beyond the horizon of most Icelanders at the time.

Introduction

i. Icelandic Narrative and Centres of Learning

Yngvar's Saga (*YS*) was probably written about the beginning
of the thirteenth century. It is a translation into Icelandic of
a now lost Latin work, which we may call *Vita Yngvari (an
asterisk indicates a lost original), by the Benedictine monk
Odd Snorrason the Learned who belonged to the monastery
of Thingeyrar in the second half of the twelfth century. Very
little is known about him, apart from the fact that he wrote
another work in Latin, a life of King Olaf Tryggvason [d.
1000]. The original of this *Vita Olavi is also now lost (apart
from a single stanza of verse in Latin), but it survives in
two Icelandic versions. It has been argued that Odd wrote
his *Vita Olavi c. 1190, and his *Vita Yngvari can hardly
have been created much before that, probably after 1180.
One feature the title heroes had in common was that both
were presented as Christian missionaries, Olaf in Norway,
Iceland and other Norse-speaking settlements in the west,
and Yngvar somewhere in Russia or ever farther to the
east. Other Icelandic narratives about missionaries include
the *Saga of Olaf the Saint* and the *Story of Thorvald the Far-
Traveller* both of which will be considered briefly below. In
the final chapter of *YS* the translator (whom we prefer to call
the saga author) gives the following account of its genesis:

> We have heard this story told, but in writing it
> down we have followed a book composed by the
> learned monk Odd, which he based on the authority
> of well-informed people mentioned by him in his letter
> to Jon Loftsson and Gizur Hallsson. Those who believe
> they know better must augment the account wherever
> they think it wanting. The monk Odd says he heard
> this story told by a priest called Isleif, and also by
> someone called Glum Thorgeirsson, and he had a third
> informant named Thorir. Odd took from each of these
> whatever he thought most interesting [*merkiligast*]. Isleif
> told him that he had heard it at the royal court of Swe-
> den. Glum had the story from his father, Thorir from
> Klakka Samsson, while Klakka learnt it from his older
> kinsmen.

Here it is suggested (a) that in the author's time, early in the
thirteenth century, there were still oral stories about Yngvar
and his expedition circulating in Iceland, although the saga

2

writer preferred the authority of a Latin text from the pen of the learned monk Odd Snorrason; (b) that Odd knew three separate informants who also could tell him something about the oral transmission preceding them; particularly interesting if the reference to the priest Isleif who got the story from someone who actually had heard it at the royal court of Sweden. Were there still members of the Swedish royal family in the middle of the twelfth century who cherished the memory of a talented, tragic kinsman, who had penetrated deeper than any other Scandinavian before him into the mysterious territories of the east? (c) that as often happens with oral transmission, there were probably as many versions as there were informants. However the saga author did not attempt to trace any part of the story back directly to the Icelander Ketil, who had accompanied Yngvar on the expedition, then come back to Sweden to describe the events and finally returned to his native land, and according to the saga 'was the first to tell of these events', (chs. 5, 8, 14). We cannot tell to what extent Odd Snorrason actually used his oral sources, but a good deal of the saga material came from books rather than native story-tellers. While the reference to oral informants may be quite genuine, it is impossible to infer from the text precisely what he had been told about Yngvar before composing his *Vita Yngvari. Yet it seems that Odd's three informants knew something memorable about an outstanding Swede called Yngvar who undertook a long arduous journey, by waterway and portage, deep into unknown territories in the east. The hazards and hardships facing the intrepid explorer were still remembered; though the geography is hazy beyond recognition, individual features of the landscape seem real enough, and it is quite possible that unidentifiable places like the whirlpool Gapi and the waterfall Belgsoti contain vague memories of actual locations.[1] It also seems that Yngvar's four named companions may have been actual people. The names are suggestive: two, the Icelander Ketil, and Soti, have Norse names; but Valdimar is Russian and Hjalmvigi probably Low German. (See Hofmann, 1981, p.194; Shepard, p.268). The principle reason why the learned monk undertook the task of composing his *Vita Yngvari must have been that the oral tradition presented Yngvar as a Christian missionary. Odd Snorrason probably found the oral accounts he had been given of Yngvar inadequate for his purposes, so he borrowed appropriate material from the world of book-learning. The idea of making Yngvar go in search of the source of a river may well have come from the imaginative and literary mind of Odd himself.

Here as elsewhere, we must make a sharp distinction between story-telling on the one hand and saga-writing on the other. In oral stories, ideas would be subordinated to the narrative flow. Each story-teller would to a large degree imitate earlier narrators, although exceptional practitioners of the art might make certain improvements and innovations. Inherent in the oral tradition about past events was a potential conflict between telling a good story and telling it in accordance with known facts. In such a situation there was always the risk that the pleasures of art might prevail. Written sagas, on the other hand, were created by educated men who would draw on a literary tradition, including Latin narrative, and would be much more concerned with the play of ideas within a consciously structured story; such authors may demonstrate their sophistication in various ways, for example in their treatment of geography, which in spite of the author's efforts may often prove to be wrong. There is another problem often overlooked by saga commentators. An illiterate Icelander in medieval times could be well informed about the past without necessarily being a story-teller; narrative was not the only form in which memories of past years were orally transmitted from one generation to another. Lists of names could be memorised, sometimes aided by mnemonics, or verse-forms, unattached to narrative. In his *Islendingabók* (written c.1125), Ari Thorgilsson the Learned gives the names of several oral informants, and there is nothing to suggest that any of them was a narrator of stories. They knew certain dates, names and other relevant facts about the short history of Iceland covered by *Islendingabók* (870–1118), but it was the responsibility of Ari himself to arrange and locate those facts in planning his history. Notwithstanding the claim in *YS* that the story had been told by several people, it is difficult to single out specific details in *YS* which must have come from oral narratives. Though the reference to Odd's informants shows that in the late twelfth century there were people who knew something about Yngvar and his expedition to the east, to this information he added materials he had gathered elsewhere.

4

So while Odd claimed that his *Vita Yngvari was based on information taken from oral tradition, and the unknown author of *Yngvar's Saga* asserts that oral stories about the title hero were still circulating in his time, the 'popular' elements remain very elusive. What is clear is that *YS* includes many features borrowed from the world of book-learning, which must have belonged to the original *Vita. All considered, it seems likely that while *YS* followed Odd's *Vita fairly closely, the final chapter and certain other details originated with the saga author rather than with the learned Odd himself.

The fact that Odd Snorrason submitted his Latin *Vita Yngvari to two known authorities is significant in the context of Icelandic learning. Jon Loftsson (d.1197) of Oddi, was grandson of Iceland's first historian, Sæmund Sigfusson the Learned (1056–1133, who, like Odd Snorrason, wrote in Latin). Jon was fosterfather to Snorri Sturluson (*c.*1178–1241), the author of *Edda, Heimskringla, Egil's Saga,* and *Olaf the Saint's Saga.* Jon Loftsson's family seat at Oddi in Rangarvellir (founded by his great-grandfather) was one of the principal intellectual centres of medieval Iceland; its reputation rested partly on its learning, partly on its school. The Oddi family took a special interest in the history of the kings of Norway. There was a particular reason for this, Jon Loftsson's mother being a natural daughter of King Magnus Bare-Legs (d.1103). This connection is stressed in the anonymous poem *Noregs konungs tal* ('Succession of the Kings of Norway') written *c.*1190 and dedicated to Jon Loftsson. More important in this respect, however, is Snorri Sturluson's *Heimskringla*, which traces the history of the kings of Norway from Odin himself down to AD 1177. Snorri came to Oddi at the age of three and received his formal education there. Furthermore, it has been argued that both *Orkneyinga Saga* ('History of the Earls of Orkney') and *Skjöldunga Saga* (which dealt with the legendary history of Denmark) were written by authors associated with Oddi.[2]

The other scholar to whom Odd Snorrason submitted his *Vita Yngvari, Gizur Hallsson (1126–1206), belonged to the family of Haukadal, another major intellectual centre and school in the south of Iceland, where Iceland's first historian in the vernacular, Ari Thorgilsson the Learned (1068–1148), was reared and educated. Gizur was an author in his own right, although his *Flos peregrinationis* ('Flower of a Pilgrimage') about his travels in Southern Europe is now lost. He may have been the compiler of *Veraldar Saga* ('History of the World'), and elsewhere he is referred to as a reliable authority on the past. Gizur was reared and educated by successive bishops of Skalholt, and was associated with the episcopal seat for most of his long life. He served as the Lawspeaker of the Althing 1181–1202, made many trips abroad and is said to have been more highly esteemed in Rome than any other Icelander before him.[3] Odd Snorrason was not the only writer to submit his work to Gizur Hallsson. Towards the end of the twelfth century Gunnlaug Leifsson wrote another *Vita Olavi, and sent the book to Gizur who kept it for two years before returning it to Gunnlaug who amended it as Gizur had suggested.[4]

The intellectual background of Odd Snorrason's *Vita Yngvari would be inadequately described without reference to the literary activity within the walls of the Thingeyrar monastery in his time. Two of his near-contemporaries there made significant contributions to early Icelandic letters. Abbot Karl Jonsson (d.1206) compiled in the vernacular the remarkable *Sverris Saga*, a detailed and authoritative biography of King Sverrir of Norway (d.1202). We have already mentioned brother Gunnlaug Leifsson (d.1219) who wrote a biography in Latin of King Olaf Tryggvason, but a much longer one than Odd Snorrason's and more ambitious; the Latin original is lost though certain parts of it survive in translation. Another Latin work from the hand of Gunnlaug was a biography of bishop Jón Ögmundarson of Holar (d. 1121); the original is lost, but three Icelandic versions of *Jóns saga biskups* are still extant. Yet another work by Gunnlaug is *The Story of Thorvald the Far-Traveller* (see below, p.25). Although his reputation as an author rested principally on his Latin writings, Gunnlaug's mastery of his native tongue can be seen from his powerful *Merlínusspá*, a metrical rendering of Geoffrey of Monmouth's *Prophecies of Merlin*. The poem is included in *Breta sogur*, the Icelandic version of Geoffrey's *Historia Regum Britanniae*.

Although *YS* alleges that certain 'learned men' had described Yngvar's expedition, there is no reason to believe that anyone apart from Odd himself had actually written

Introduction

about these events before the saga author came along. Yet
YS includes several features which evidently derive from
European learning and had nothing to do with oral tales
about Yngvar and his journey to the east. First, there is
the reference to the *Gesta Saxonum* (ch. 14) which in fact
is the *History of the Bishops of the Church of Hamburg* by
Adam of Bremen (d.*c*.1081). Second, several place names
in the east derive from medieval authorities, such as Isidore
of Seville (d.636). Scitopolis/Citopolis (ch. 8) has been
identified with Scythopolis in Palestine. It is not known
where Odd Snorrason got it from, but there are references
to Scythopolis in 2 Maccabees and elsewhere. Heliopolis
(chs. 5 and 7) could have been borrowed from Isidore.[5]
Two cities by that name are mentioned in early sources,
one in Lower Egypt, the other in Lebanon. The headland
Siggeum was situated on the Asiatic side of the Hellespont.[6]
Such phenomena as the *Cyclopes* (ch. 9)[7] are obviously borrowed from books and there is no reason to doubt that the
flying dragon Jaculus comes from a learned source rather
than the native tradition. It is tempting to assume that Odd
Snorrason borrowed it either from Isidore[8] or directly from
his source Lucan (IX. 720). The Icelandic *Rómverja saga* (a
translation of selected passages from Lucan's *Civil War* and
Sallust's *The War with Catalina* and *The War with Jugurtha*),
which appears to date from the same period as *YS* includes
an expanded description of the Jaculus. The description of
the giant 'with a large number of men dangling from his belt'
(ch. 6) suggests an *anthropophagus* or maneater.[9] It is of course
possible that such learned elements in *YS* may derive from
other authorities than Isidore, and there are indeed certain
features in *YS* not mentioned here which suggest the author's
book-learning. In this connection it is interesting to note that
another saga-writer describing distant regions felt obliged to
borrow from learned sources. The author of *Eirik's Saga*
probably got the idea of unipeds, one-legged hopping men,
from Isidore, when he included them among the natives of
Vinland (America). In *YS*, the world is supposed to end near
the Red Sea. Elsewhere (e.g. in *Stjórn*), the end of the world
is located east of India.

Eymund's Saga (*ES*) is evidently much younger than *YS*
which served as one its sources, as will be discussed later.

Robert Cook (1986: p.71) thinks it was written in the fourteenth century, but does not indicate how much older it is than the MS containing it (*c*.1380). It may be older. We can see no reason why it could not have been written even as early as the latter part of the thirteenth century. It is anonymous, and the only thing we know about its origin is what we can infer from the saga itself. *ES* opens with a brief mention of a certain provincial king in eleventh-century Norway; Hring Dagsson ruler of Hringariki (now Ringerike), a descendant of King Harald Finehair. Notwithstanding some glaring discrepancies, we are evidently dealing with the same person as Hring Dagsson who ruled over Heidmarken about the same time. It seems probable that the author of *ES* deliberately substituted *Hring*ariki for Heidmarken for the simple reason that it suited the king's name better. But another deviation is more significant: according to *ES* this Hring had three sons, all destined to become kings, namely Hrærek, Eymund and Dag. But according to *Heimskringla* and other early sources about Norway in the time of St Olaf (d.1030), Hring and his *brother* Hrærek were joint rulers of Heidmarken, and there is no reference prior to *ES* to either Hrærek or *Eymund* as *sons* of Hring, though Dag Hringsson figures in the last section of *The Saga of St Olaf* in *Heimskringla* and elsewhere. So whereas *ES* presents Hrærek as Hring's son, he appears as his brother in other accounts. There is not a shred of evidence that the author of *ES* knew any written or oral stories about *Eymund Hringsson*, the title hero of the saga and this character appears to be an invention of the author himself. So when we find references in the *Flateyjarbók* version of *The Saga of St Olaf* to Eymund 'King Olaf's bloodbrother' we are evidently dealing with influences on that work from *ES*. This assumption that the redactor of *Olaf's Saga* in *Flateyjarbók* used *ES* seems reasonable enough, since the same scribe copied both sagas in *Flateyjarbók*. Although the saga character Eymund Hringsson appears to have been invented by the author of *ES*, one can guess where he got the hero's name. In an old genealogy, preserved in several works, *Lay of Hyndla*, *Snorra Edda* and *How Norway Was Won*, there is a reference to a king called '*Eymund*' who was associated with Holmgard (i.e. Novgorod) and whose daughter married a legendary king called Hálfdan the Old. This Eymund may have provided the author of *ES* with the name of the title hero. This would not be the first time that a saga author borrowed a name from another source. We may note that Eymund's bloodbrother Ragnar Agnarsson must be another invention by the author, notwithstanding the echoing genealogy in ch. 1: 'Ragnar, son of Agnar, who was the son of Ragnar Rykkil, son of Harald Fine-hair.' Such genealogies served to give credence to an unhistorical personage. It is tempting to assume that the author of *ES* may have modelled the heroic sounding name Ragnar Agnarsson on Agnar Ragnarsson, the valiant warrior in the *Saga of Ragnar Hairy-Breeks*.

There is no apparent reason to assume that the author of *ES* used Snorri Sturluson's *Saga of St Olaf*, but the reference to Styrmir the Learned (ch. 1) shows clearly that he must have known Snorri's principal source, Styrmir Karason's *Saga of Olaf*, of which numerous fragments survive in *Flateyjarbók* and elsewhere. The statement in *ES* about St Olaf – 'According to Styrmir the Learned the story is that he dethroned eleven kings in Norway, five of them on a single morning.' – corresponds precisely to two of the extant fragments of Styrmir's work. Styrmir Karason (d.1245) was one of the outstanding intellectuals of medieval Iceland, combining foreign learning with the study of the history of Iceland and Norway. In addition to the *Saga of St Olaf*, he also compiled a now lost version of the *Book of Settlements* and made a copy of Karl Jonsson's *Sverrir's Saga*. In *Hord's Saga* he is referred to as an authority on the life of that celebrated outlaw. Styrmir was a priest by training; he acted as the Lawspeaker of the Althing 1210–14 and 1232–35. For the last ten years of his life (1235–45) he was Prior in the Augustinian House on Videy, which was founded by Snorri Sturluson and Thorvald Gizurarson in 1226. In the small world of thirteenth-century Iceland it is not surprising to find that Styrmir and Snorri were close friends as well as fellow authors.

There are cross-currents between *ES* and *YS* indicating that the former is borrowing from and embroidering upon the latter. The author of *ES* appears to conflate two figures, both Ingigerd's cousins: Earl Rognvald from the *Saga of Olaf the Saint*, and Eymund Akason from *Yngvar's Saga*. In both Styrmir's biography of St Olaf and Snorri Sturluson's *Heimskringla*, we are told that 'Queen Ingigerd gave Rognvald Ladoga Town and the region that went with it. Rognvald was earl there for a long time, and was an outstanding man.' (*Heimskringla II*, 148; the same statement is to be found in *Flateyjarbók* immediately before *Eymund's Saga*.) In *ES*, presumably with this in mind, the author tells us that Ingigerd announced 'Earl Rognvald was to rule over Ladoga Town as he had done in the past', the last phrase seeming to assume the reader's knowledge of events recorded in Styrmir's biography of St Olaf. But *ES* also tells us something that is not in Styrmir, writing of Queen Ingigerd and Earl Rognvald 'between whom there was a secret affair', the last sentence of the saga, undeveloped, casual and contextually unrelated. It could refer to an unknown source, but more likely is that it derives from *YS* (ch.2) where Ingigerd and Eymund are said to have been very much in love with one another, and that when he was wounded in a fight with her father's men 'she drove him home and healed him in secret'. *Yngvar's Saga* mentions Ingigerd's marriage to Jarisleif; 'when Eymund Akason heard the news he travelled to Russia in order to visit them, and Jarisleif and Ingigerd welcomed him warmly' (ch. 3); this may have given rise to the sentence in *ES* about a love affair between Rognvald and Ingigerd, since *ES* may have confused Rognvald with Eymund Akason of *YS*, and taken over Eymund's name for its hero. In *YS* Eymund has good reasons for going to Russia to visit a close friend from the past and her new husband, but *YS* suggests no sexual relationship between the two after their early love affair. In *ES*, Eymund Hringsson has no particular reason to go to Russia except that he has heard that there are political tensions and there may be work for him as a mercenary. However, once in Russia, Eymund Hringsson of *ES* behaves in much the same manner as Eymund Akason in *YS*: both help King Jarisleif against his brother Burislaf. In *ES* this is Eymund Hringsson's essential role which occupies most of the story, but *YS* (ch. 3) devotes only a brief paragraph to Eymund Akason's military intervention in the east: 'At that time Russia was in a state of war, for Burislaf, King Jarisleif's brother was making attacks on the kingdom. Eymund fought against him in five battles, and in the last battle Burislaf was captured, blinded, and brought before the king. . . . Meanwhile, Eymund was in Novgorod fighting many a battle, always gaining the victory, and recovering for the king tributary territories.'

ii. The Narratives

Yngvar's Saga tells the story of a disinherited Swedish prince who sets out from his native shore looking for a new realm in a distant land, but then changes his aim and undertakes the most romantic kind of quest, a perilous journey across mysterious regions in search of the source of a great river. The hero's pilgrimage into the unknown, with all its natural wonders, wealth and temptations, including seductive women, constitutes the main part of the saga. But this central panel of the triptych is flanked by minor ones; it is preceded by an introductory section dealing with Yngvar's family and youth, and followed by a second journey undertaken by his surviving natural son, Svein. The first section (chs. 1–4) explains Yngvar's relationship to the royal house of Sweden and the reasons for his failure to attain a throne. It is possible that Odd Snorrason got some of the historical details in this part of the saga from written sources; there is indeed some overlap with the *Olaf's Saga* which is based on his *Vita Olavi. There is no reference to Yngvar elsewhere in the saga literature, apart from the following passage in *Gongu-Hrolf's Saga*: 'King Hreggvid . . . had won territory beyond the River Dvina that flows through Russia; from there he had raided various nations to the east and taken from them many a rare treasure. This river is the third or fourth biggest in the world and it was to find its source that Yngvar the Far-Travelled set out, as told in his saga.'[10] But the stuff that went into the making of the central panel and its sequel derives partly at least from foreign learning, as we have seen. Considering the fantastic elements in the description of Yngvar's expedition, historians and other scholars would certainly have rejected the whole account as sheer invention by the saga author, if there had been no corroborative evidence available.[11] But as it happens, no one is likely to call into question the claim that Yngvar undertook such a journey, even if a good many descriptive details of the saga have little to do with historical fact. There are at least twenty-two runic inscriptions in Sweden commemorating men who accompanied Yngvar to the east.[12]

At the outset the title hero of *Eymund's Saga* is a young practising viking whose father is forced to surrender his provincial kingdom in Norway when King Olaf comes

11

to the throne. Young Eymund goes east to Russia where three brothers, Burislaf of Kiev, Jarisleif of Novgorod, and Vartilaf of Polotsk are at loggerheads with one another over territorial claims. To begin with, Eymund offers his services to Jarisleif, but later transfers his loyalty to his brother Vartilaf. Eymund's role is a variant of a well-know topos: a young warrior (typically eighteen years of age) visits a strange country and successfully defends the realm against enemy attack. Here, we may note three examples: in *Olaf's Tryggvason's Saga* the title hero who was actually brought up in Russia defends the kingdom for Jarisleif's father: 'King Valdimar appointed him commander over the troops he dispatched to defend his realm. Olaf fought several battles and proved a skilful leader of the army.' But as sometimes happens in such circumstances, people envied Olaf and slandered him to the king, so the young defender had to leave the country. *Bjorn's Saga* tells of a young Icelander who travels to Russia and stays with King Valdimar over the winter. Then a huge army led by King Valdimar's close kinsman Kaldimar, (evidently an invented name, a variation of Valdimar) suddenly arrives on the scene and threatens national security. The Russians are helpless and there is no telling what would have happened if young Bjorn had not averted the impending disaster by killing Kaldimar in single combat. The fictitious tale *Egil and Asmund* tells of two young warriors, one a king's son from Halogaland in Norway, the other a prince from Smaland in Sweden. They become joint defenders of Russia for the legendary King Hertrygg, and everyone feels safe as long as they are in charge.

In his important study of *Eymund's Saga*, Robert Cook has compared the saga to the account in the *Primary Chronicle* of Russian events during the period 1015–1034. He correctly identifies Jarisleif with King Yaroslav who came to the throne in 1015, but his identification of Jarisleif's brothers, Burislaf and Vartilaf is more problematic. Cook argues that Burislaf represents Yaroslav's half-brother Svyatapolk, and that the name Burislaf was borrowed from Svyatapolk's father-in-law, Boleslav. But what about the third brother, Vartilaf, whose name is unknown outside *ES*? Robert Cook finds an ingenious solution to the problem: 'The figure of Vartilaf in the tale represents a conflation of two characters in the

Chronicle: Bryachislaf, from whom come the name Vartilaf and the place of residence Polotsk/Palteskja, and Mstislav who, like the Vartilaf in the tale, made a peaceful settlement with Yaroslav and then died obligingly early, leaving his portion of the realm to Yaroslav.' Cook assumes that the historical matter in *ES* was transmitted orally; that 'Eymund' and his men actually took part in certain campaigns and battles during the period 1016–1024; and that 'survivors of this experience (though not Eymund himself, who stayed in Russia) returned to Scandinavia, if not to Iceland, carrying tales of their adventures with them' (p.71). But as we noted earlier, the account of the Russian campaigns in *ES* is partly based on written sources going back to the late twelfth century, Odd Snorrason's *Vita Yngvari, (Yngvar's Saga)*, and the *Saga of St Olaf*. And there appears no reason to assume that the author of *ES* had access to any orally transmitted stories about the people and events involved. Recurrent topoi and motifs are discussed by Cook and point to the inescapable conclusion that *ES*, far from being a historical record, is a construct of conventional material. The author 'put the saga together', from all the sundry materials he could lay his hands on. As we said earlier, the title hero of *ES* appears to be modelled on his namesake Eymund in *YS* who successfully defend's Jarisleif's kingdom against the aggression of his brother Burislaf. Since the author of *ES* had an obvious predilection for triads he simply added the third brother, Vartilaf.[13] *ES* makes no reference to oral sources, which, in the circumstances is not surprising; Eymund's conventional role as 'a young defender' is a stock motif in literature and belongs to the art of saga-writing rather than to history or historical tradition. Regretfully, we believe that Robert Cook's resourceful attempt to square *ES* with Russian history carries less conviction than his demonstration of its dependence on topoi and recurrent popular motifs.

Another commentator, Jonathan Shepard, has carefully examined the historical relevance of *Yngvar's Saga*. He reviews various theories identifying Yngvar's host with the one that attacked Byzantium in 1043, another which attacked the Arab Emirs in the Caucasus in the early 1030s. Mats Larsson has recently advanced the hypothesis that Yngvar's host was the one recorded in the Georgian Chronicle as having aided King Bagrat IV in the defence of his throne in a civil war against a chieftain, Liparit, who wished to set up Bagrat's half-brother, Demetrius, on the throne of Georgia. Bagrat was defeated in the Battle of Sasireti, the date of which has been argued as between 1041 and 1046. The Scandinavians fought bravely, being the only troops of Bagrat not to run from the battlefield. They were taken captive and well and honourably treated by Liparit, ultimately being released to make their way back home. Shepard rejects this identification, but what these speculations show is the persistent involvement of Scandinavian warrior-bands in the region of Georgia and the Caspian during the early to mid-eleventh century. Shepard discusses an ancient Russian stone cross set up 'near a land-and-water route from the Caspian to the Sea of Azov', which is now barely legible but according to an eighteenth-century informant was dated 1041, which Shepard argues might be linked, very speculatively, he admits, with Yngvar's expedition, pointing out that the eastern route to Byzantium was being increasingly used in the eleventh century, so that 'travel between Kievian Russia and Byzantium was common and comparatively rapid.' Shepard, p.225. (For connections between Viking Russia and Byzantium, see Dennis Ward's article.)[14] Although the date of Yngvar's death in *Konungsannáll*, *YS* itself, and the numerous runic inscriptions mentioned above serve to show that Yngvar's expedition must have taken place, it has proved impossible to point to a single Russian source that unequivocally refers to this event. Indeed, it would have been a remarkable thing if Russian or Georgian chroniclers had mentioned the tragic Yngvar, whose real achievements were probably much less memorable than *YS* suggests.

iii. Characterisation and Literary Roles

As we indicated earlier, apart from the business of entertainment, one of the purposes of the sagas was to teach audiences something about themselves: a good saga would throw light not only on people from the past, but on human nature in general or as interpreted in the present. The author might indeed show at times a healthy scepticism which in its way offered a significant message to the audience about how to understand story-telling. For example, there is a cheerful disclaimer of elevated motives at the end of *Göngu-Hrolfs Saga*, itself a fantasy about heroic adventures in Russia, which takes for its title the name of the historical figure Göngu–Hrolf (Rollo), the Scandinavian founder of the Duchy of Normandy. It offers very little that could be called historical, though it is packed with the kind of human, often comic observation to be expected of the genial author who tells us at the close of his tale:

> . . .The story goes that Hrolf lived to a ripe old age, but it's not stated whether he died in his bed or was killed with weapons.
>
> Now even if there are discrepancies between this story and others dealing with the same events, such as names and other details, and what individual people achieved by greatness or wisdom or witchcraft or treachery, it's still most likely that those who wrote and composed this narrative must have had something to go on, either old poems or the records of learned men. There are certainly very few stories about ancient people, perhaps none, which one would like to swear to be the literal truth, because most of them have been more or less exaggerated. And it's impossible to prove the truth of every word and incident in some of the episodes, because most things described clearly occur later than they're supposed to. But it's best not to cast aspersions on this or call the stories of learned men lies, unless one can tell the stories more plausibly and in a more elegant way. Old stories and poems are offered more as entertainments of the moment than as eternal truths. There are a few things told that can't be put in doubt by some old example to the contrary, and it's said in all truth that God has given the heathen wisdom and understanding of worldly things, along with outstanding bravery, wealth and physical beauty, just as he has Christians.
>
> So here we must end this tale of Hrolf Sturlaugsson and his great exploits. I'd like to thank those who've listened and enjoyed the story, and since those who don't like it won't ever be satisfied, let them enjoy their own misery. AMEN

Implicit in this author's deceptively offhand approach is his confidence that his audience will be on the watch for the questions raised by the tale and the motives of the teller. When he expresses his doubts about the seeker of 'literal truth', he invites the reader's participation in the interpretation of the tale's purposes not as a factual record, but in terms of its own particular literary kind.

Yngvar's Saga could be described as a quest romance. When he leaves Sweden, frustrated by his failure to fulfil his ambition to rule, Yngvar seeks 'a kingdom in some foreign land' (Ch. 4). This goal is never achieved, though his meeting with Queen Silkisif makes it a distinct possibility, but he dies before it is realised. He becomes obsessed with the discovery of the source of a great river, a unique goal in early Icelandic literature. The only other quest-romance that comes to mind in this connection is the *Saga of Eirik the Far-Traveller*, whose hero undertakes a journey to the Orient in search of Paradise on earth. Yngvar reaches the source of his river, then dies before he can return to marry Queen Silkisif. After his death, his role is taken over by his natural son, Svein, who marries Silkisif and thus completes the initial ambitious enterprise of his father.

In *YS*, as elsewhere, the role of a quest maker is a simple one, and lacking in sophistication to say the least. Yngvar is a precocious lad who at the tender age of nine sets out on a grand tour of Sweden, escorted by 'fourteen other men each one in armour, bearing a shield, and riding armoured horses. They wore gilded helmets and all their weapons were embellished with silver and gold'. His great achievement as a youthful hero is to reconcile his father and the King of Sweden who, though first cousins, are at loggerheads. In order to achieve this, Yngvar uses a method which features in *Egil's Saga* and elsewhere: he brings a splendid gift to the king claiming it comes from his father, and then he gives his father another fine present saying it is from the king. Both recipients suspect the truth but the ruse helps to create the right atmosphere for the restoration of amity between the kinsmen. But this does not help Yngvar's own position, for the King of Sweden persistently refuses to give him the title of king, even after Yngvar has served him with great distinction. Yngvar appears to have inherited some of his family's lucklessness. His grandfather Aki was killed by his own father-in-law, so Yngvar's father, Eymund, was brought up by his father's killer who was also his maternal grandfather. For a while Eymund is outlawed from Sweden by the king, his cousin. The only human happiness in Eymund's life appears to be brought into it by his cousin Ingigerd: they fall in love and she saves his life, essential ingredients of the characteristic quest of the romances, the love-search. Even so, here the love theme is abruptly dropped and Ingigerd is married to King Jarisleif of Russia. After some time, Eymund visits her and takes charge of Russia's defences, taking on the conventional role of the young defender.

In the sagas it is a common practice to give a formal description of the hero (conventional in that such descriptions are often very similar), either when he is introduced, or at some crucial point in his life. In Yngvar's case this point comes just before he sets out to suppress a rebellion against King Olaf, in whose service he is at the time:

> Yngvar was a tall, handsome man, strong and fair-complexioned. He was shrewd and well-spoken, kind and generous to his friends, ruthless to his enemies, a courteous man and always correct in his conduct: as a result, wise men have often compared him to his kinsman Styrbjorn, and to King Olaf Tryggvason, the most famous in the eyes of God and men ever to come out of Scandinavia, or who ever will to the end of time. (ch. 3).

The comparison with Styrbjorn and Olaf is interesting not so much because it suggests certain qualities in Yngvar himself, but rather because it invites the reader to think of particular sagas and saga heroes. Yngvar and Olaf had several striking features in common; apart from their missionary activities, both are Vikings, both show the same kind of ruthlessness and resolve, which is not so surprising considering the fact that *Yngvar's saga* and the earliest version of *Olafs saga Tryggvasonar* are translations of Latin works by the same author, Odd Snorrason. In Odd's *Olafs' saga* there is a brief reference to Styrbjorn who is described there as the most valiant of men and an exceptional fighter. He fought against King Eirik the Victorious of Sweden, who figures in the first chapters of *YS* and is said to be Yngvar's great-grandfather. Also there is a separate narrative about him, the so-called *Styrbjarnar páttur Svíakappa* ('The Story of Styrbjorn the Champion of the Swedes'). According to that story, Styrbjorn was King Eirik's nephew and fosterson. After killing one of the king's retainers, called Aki, Styrbjorn is barred from the throne he was entitled to and banished from Sweden. He goes on a viking expedition to the east, and eventually he is killed in battle, fighting against the troops of his uncle and fosterfather, King Eirik of Sweden, the man who had his son-in-law, Aki, put to death in *YS*. There seems to be some connection between these two stories, but it is difficult to decide how their affinities should be explained.

Once the nature of Yngvar's quest has shifted, from an earlier preoccupation with getting worldly power and a kingdom to rule, towards finding out 'the length of this river' and converting the heathen, the characters in the saga appear to be placed in two camps. There are those who help him attain his goal, his loyal companions, and on the other hand his enemies, the swarm of monsters, giants, dragons and demons. But the lines are in fact not quite so simply drawn. The most dangerous of his enemies are displayed in the form of the very heathen he wishes to convert, in particular the seductive women, one of whom is Silkisif the Queen of the land, with whom a highly ambivalent relationship is to develop.

When we write of 'character' with reference to figures in these sagas, we do not see them as developing in the way character is to be found in the great sagas, for instance in Gudrun, the powerful dominant woman of *Laxdæla Saga*, or Snorri in *Eyrbyggja Saga*, whom Sir Walter Scott saw as comparable to figures in the European novel.[15] Romance figures have much more in common with the folktale, in which they are used to explore situations rather than the individual, but this is not to say that they lack complexity, depth and interest. The saga author may use such figures to elaborate upon problematic human situations which, as in fairy tales, have been recognised as bearing not only upon the world of the child, but that of the adult confronting essential paradoxes in dilemmas within his society and his own personality. Consequently, 'characters' are usually 'types' associated with recurrent themes or 'topoi'. The male figure of 'the young defender' is one such, and the female type of the 'threatening seductress' is another, developed largely in terms of the inner and outer problems of the male hero in the figure here of Queen Silkisif.

We have discussed the 'temptress' in some detail elsewhere[16], and in Icelandic Romances she is often an ambiguous figure associated with the equally ambiguous

King Godmund of 'Shining Plains' (*Glasisvellir*), the mythical heathen magician who rules over a remote Siberian (?) wasteland of snow and ice, sometimes figuring as a threat, sometimes a friend and an accomplice. His female counterpart, for example his daughter Ingibjorg in *Helgi Thorisson*, has affinities with a recurrent figure in European folklore, such as the fairy woman who seduced Thomas the Rhymer in the ballad which was one of the sources of Keat's 'La Belle Dame Sans Merci'. The woman also furnishes Thomas with special knowledge of the underworld to which she takes him. The pattern usually begins with the hero meeting a group of women, one of whom is exceptionally beautiful and distinguished-looking. Significantly, Thomas the Rhymer first mistakes her identity, calling her 'the Queen of Heaven', but she rapidly disabuses him of this error by declaring herself the Queen of Faery, and inviting him to bed, an offer which neither Thomas nor his Icelandic counterpart Helgi find it possible to refuse. In *Yngvar's Saga* (ch. 5) when 'this fine lady beckoned Yngvar and his men to come and meet her', the hero, already established in the apparently contradictory roles of Christian missionary and viking predator, is less forthcoming, refusing at first even to speak to the 'temptress', and when in due course he does go with her to her city he forbids his men to 'mix with the heathen or allow any woman into the hall apart from the queen'. After they have had conversation, she falls in love with him and agrees to embrace Christianity, offering to share her realm with him; he refuses since he is now committed to his travels up-river, no longer a straightforward viking expedition but a search for beginnings and a Christian mission or crusade. Yngvar continues to warn his men against defiling themselves 'by having affairs with women or any other kind of heathen practice' and the pattern of the seduction of the hero in the type-tale is being altered here. Since the original 'temptress' figure, Silkisif, has as it were, changed moral sides, it is necessary for the story-teller to introduce an alternative 'beautiful seductress'. Yngvar continues his journey, and after a while into his camp marches a band of women, led by the usual 'lady of most quality', who declares her intention of sleeping with him, 'which so enraged him he drew out his knife and stabbed her in the private parts. When the other men saw what he had done, some began chasing their loose women away, but there were others who slept with them, unable to resist their seductive charms and devilish witchcraft' (ch. 7). Both the virtuous Christian resistance to temptation and the violent impulse of the male viking world are brought out here in uneasy relationship, over which the monastic author has equally uneasy control in his rehandling of the basic seduction tale. But the hand of evil has touched Yngvar and though he and his men race back to Silkisif, the army has been striken with disease through contact with the devilish aliens, and Yngvar himself is dying. He declares that 'it is by the righteous judgement of God that I have been stricken with this disease' and dies. In *Helgi Thorisson*, the hero is first blinded by the temptress, then dies, while in his ballad, true Thomas returns to earth with his new knowledge, but in some versions threatened with blinding by his furious paramour.

Interestingly, the author is unable to allow Silksif to shed all traces of her origins in the folk-seductress: it is left to Svein, Yngvar's son, to marry Silkisif and briefly rule the converted kingdom with his now Christian queen, but his arrival in her kingdom sounds echoes of these pagan origins:

> [Svein] reached the land of Queen Silkisif, where she came out to meet them in grand style. After they had disembarked, Ketil was the first to greet the queen, but she paid no attention to him and turned towards Svein trying to kiss him. He pushed her away and said he had no desire to kiss her, a heathen woman.
>
> 'Anyway,' he asked, 'why should you want to kiss me?'
>
> 'Yours are the only eyes here like Yngvar's that I can see,' she replied. (ch. 12).

There is an interesting passage in another of the works of Odd Snorrason his *Saga of Olaf Tryggvason* in which occurs a fanciful account of a group of mysterious giantesses overheard swapping stories about their dealings with King Olaf, who was never known to fall victim to seductive women of any kind. One of the troll-women says:

> 'What I can tell about myself is that I assumed the appearance of a beautiful woman; in my hand I carried a horn full of mead which I had mixed with many nasty things, intending to serve it to the king in the evening, at the place where he was feasting. When the men had got

20

very drunk, and I stood there beside the table beautifully dressed, the king stretched out his hand to me, and I went up to him giving him the horn. But he raised the horn aloft and drove in onto my head and right against my face, and that was the end of our dealings.'

But another troll-woman told a story more to the point:

'I assumed the form of a beautiful woman, and went to the king's chambers late one evening. The king was there, barefoot and with his linen pants tied round the leg. The bishop was sitting on his right hand side. Then I started making the king feel itchy in the foot, and when he noticed me standing there, he called to me asking me to alleviate the itchiness in his foot, so I sat down on the foot-stool beside him both before supper and after. When the king went to bed and I with him, I kept scratching his foot. First the bishop fell asleep, then the king, and I tried to destroy the king with devilish tricks. Then the king woke up and struck me on the head with a book, smashing my skull. With that I ran away, and since then I carry my head to one side.' (ch. 60).

So, not necessarily fully aware of what he reveals of the shadowy corners of the missionary experience, the author makes his revisions of the folk-material. There is little doubt that the monastic author sees his tale as also relating to the tradition of hagiography found in such works as *Orkneyinga Saga*, *Magnus' Saga*, and *Knytlinga Saga*, in which various saintly and often ex-viking heroes resist such temptations of the flesh. Indeed, Yngvar bears a close resemblance to the type of the Northern saint we have discussed elsewhere, the Holy Warrior, such as Earl Rognvald of Orkney.[17] He is another far-traveller, who begins as an acquisitive viking and then, still a man of considerable violence as well as a poet, tempted in his travels by love, makes a journey to the Holy Land where he composes this poem:

A cross on this bard's
breast, on his back
a palm-branch: peacefully
we pace the hillside.

He founded St Magnus' Cathedral in Orkney to honour his kinsman, Magnus, whose miracles were necessary to

21

prove his worthiness to a sceptical bishop. This might remind the reader of another passage in *Yngvar's Saga*, when a great church is built in honour of Yngvar and the bishop asks:

> 'In whose name, queen, do you wish this church to be dedicated?'
>
> 'This church,' she said, 'shall be dedicated to the glory of the Holy King, Yngvar, who rests here.'
>
> 'Why?' asked the bishop. 'Has Yngvar shone in miracles since his death?' [But the minister is, on Silkisif's insistence, dedicated to] 'the glory of God and all His saints, including Yngvar.'(ch. 13)

To conclude, then, though we would never claim developed characterisation for these two sagas, the handling of type-roles in certain cases is by no means insignificant. In *ES*, Eymund himself fails to develop far beyond his type, taking on the stereotypic role of the 'young defender' while the author, as Cook demonstrates convincingly, exploits popular recurrent tales. The author himself does not seem too interested when he tells us that Eymund 'lived to no great age and died peacefully', in saga terms something of the equivalent of a yawn. Jarisleif and Burislaf are largely pieces of the machinery, Jarisleif characterised by stinginess and failure to keep his word on matters of money, which has a kind of comic potential never really developed, and Burislaf by his guile, which nevertheless does not get him very far.

After Eymund has switched his allegiance and joined forces with Vartilaf, the narrator has difficulty finding any narrative direction and only manages to extricate himself from this impasse by developing Queen Ingigerd, who imposes her own will and a new order on the political situation, breathing some life into the dying narrative. Elsewhere, Ingigerd and Jarisleif act out minor roles, which might have a bearing on this development. In *St Olaf's Saga* Ingigerd is presented as a woman who know her own mind and gets what she wants, and the author of *ES* appears to develop her as a character in much the same way as *St Olaf's Saga*. In fact, in the final sentence of *ES*, the author seems to suggest that she might have made a more interesting central figure, had it been her story he was telling rather than Eymund's. Although her role and that of Silkisif in *YS* are very different, each of them is potentially a more interesting figure in terms of 'character' than most of the men in the tale.

iv. Scholars and Travellers

As we have seen already, several Icelandic authors between the late eleventh and the thirteenth centuries were given the honorific nickname 'the Learned' (*hinn fróði*). What these writers had in common was that they were assiduous explorers of the records of the past and regarded as trustworthy authorities on people and events of bygone times. Most of the Icelandic sagas from the medieval period are anonymous, so we know little about the kind of education these authors were given. The saga writers were primarily interested in individuals: the personalities, destinies, and achievements of the characters figuring in the narrative. But as we have said, a well-wrought saga was supposed not only to show the reader how certain men in the past had lived and died, but also tell him something about mankind. Saga commentators in medieval Iceland made a distinction between the two primary functions of the sagas, which were usually read aloud: to instruct and to entertain. The entertainment value differs greatly from one saga to another. In a popular adventure story, as now, suspense, love, battle, ultimate triumph and so on were essential ingredients, their delight in strange places and creatures having something in common with the science fiction of our own time. Some of the most entertaining sagas are practically devoid of historical information, and they tend to be set in distant lands and in remote, barely remembered periods. The so-called *fornaldarsögur*, 'Stories about the remote past' and *riddarasögur*, 'Chivalric Romances', belong here. At a more serious level, a good saga was intended to teach the audience about real historical personages and actual events, although the literary or entertainment value was not necessarily sacrificed to moral edification or instruction about the past. Many of the great and best known sagas are about Icelanders who belonged in the period *c*.900–*c*.1050, the *Islendingasögur*, 'Sagas of the Icelanders', such as *Njal's Saga*, *Laxdæla Saga*, *Egil's Saga*, *Grettir's Saga*, *Hrafnkel's Saga*, *Eyrbyggja Saga*, and *Gisli's Saga*. Another important group dealing with historical matters are the *konungasögur*, 'Sagas of the Kings', most of which are about the rulers of Norway from the tenth to the thirteenth centuries, but

here too belong *Knytlinga Saga*, 'The History of the Kings
of Denmark', *Orkneyinga Saga*, 'The History of the Earls
of Orkney' and *Færeyinga Saga*, 'The Faroe Islanders'
Saga'.

On the whole, the saga authors show a keen interest
in geography; even episodes involving monsters and other
fantastic elements may still convey reasonably practical and
sober views of faraway lands. In this connection it is worth
bearing in mind that the medieval Icelanders were eager to
learn everything they could about countries in Europe and
beyond; several early Icelandic treatises on geography have
been collected and edited in the first volume of *Alfræði islenzk*
('An Icelandic Encyclopedia'). Probably the most striking
piece in the whole collection is the *Leiðarvísir* of Abbot
Nikulas Bergsson (d.1159), which describes in remarkable
detail the pilgrim route from Iceland through Rome to the
Holy Land. He set out on his long journey c. 1150 returning
in 1154. Scattered throughout the sagas we find useful hints
about foreign lands, as for example the following piece in
Göngu-Hrolfs Saga:

> England is the most productive country in Western
> Europe, because all sorts of metal are worked there, and
> wines and wheat grow, and a number of different cereals
> besides. More varieties of cloth and textiles are woven
> there than in other lands. London is the principal town,
> and then Canterbury. Besides these are Scarborough,
> Hastings, Winchester, and many towns and cities not
> mentioned here. (p.22)

Such geographical knowledge derived either from actual
travellers, like Abbot Nikulas, who described their own
experience in order to guide others who wanted to leave
their native shore, or from books of foreign learning. As we
have seen, scholarly explorers of the past were given the nickname 'the Learned', but those who set out from Iceland and
explored the physical world were called 'the Far-Travellers'
(*inn víðförli*). One of the bearers of this nickname was our
hero Yngvar; an essential purpose of *YS* was to show us how
he earned that distinguished title. Other men given the nickname 'the Far-Traveller' include Thorvald Kodransson who,
after travelling widely in Europe and embracing Christianity
there, returned to Iceland with a German priest, *c*.981 and
with his help – with limited success as it turned out – tried to

convert his fellow countrymen to the Catholic faith. Several
years later he left his native shore again, never to return. He
is said to have travelled all the way to the Holy Land, and from
there to Byzantium, and then by the eastern route to Kiev up
the river Dnjepr. According to *Kristni Saga* Thorvald died in
Russia, a short distance from Polotsk:

> and there he was buried on a certain mountain at the
> Church of St John the Baptist and is considered a holy
> man. This is what Brand the Far-Traveller said:
>
> I came to where Christ
> grants Thorvald Kodransson
> His peace, the holy one,
> on the high hill
> at St John's Church, Drofn
> the dead man lies.

The account in Gunnlaug Leifsson's *Story of Thorvald
Kodransson* (see above, p.6) does not differ significantly,
which is not surprising since it was probably one of the
sources used by the compiler of *Kristni saga*. Apart from
this single reference nothing is known about Brand the
Far-Traveller. Although it has proved impossible to identify the place name *Drofn*, the tradition about Thorvald's
ultimate fate appears to be quite genuine. Similarly, there is
no apparent reason why the reference to Brand and his visit
to Russia should be treated with suspicion, although there
is no other reference to him in medieval sources. But his
verse is simply so bad that it must be genuine. The fourth
person honoured with the nickname 'the Far-Traveller' is
the eponymous hero of the fictitious *Eiriks saga víðförlia*, a
Christian tale about a prince in pagan Norway who swears a
solemn vow one Christmas Eve to travel all over the world
in search of 'the place the heathen called Odainsakur [Field
of Eternal Life], and the Christians The Land of the Living
or Paradise'. Eirik travels to Byzantium where he helps the
Emperor fight his enemies ('the young defender' motif yet
again), and from him Eirik learns that Paradise lies east of
the remotest part of India. From Byzantium Eirik makes his
way east through Syria and then onward to India and beyond,
eventually attaining his pledged goal. Whether or not there
ever was a real personage called Eirik the Far-Traveller is
hard to say, though if he never existed, the saga narrator
would have had little difficulty in inventing him. The claim in

Introduction

Halfdan Eysteinsson (ch. 1) that Eirik was the great-grandson
of Odin is hardly evidence for his existence, though it serves
to show that the author of *Halfdan Eysteinsson* must have read
The Saga of Eirik the Far-Traveller. The fifth notable bearer
of the nickname is the eponymous hero of *Arrow-Odd*, who
visited many parts of Europe including Permia and other
regions in Russia. It can hardly be a mere coincidence that all
these five bearers of the nickname are said to have travelled in
the east, four of them actually in Russia itself. In *Arrow-Odd*
there is an interesting description of Russia, an extraordinary
mixture of geography and fantasy (ch. 30):

> Russia is a vast country, with a number of different
> kingdoms. There was a king called Marro who ruled
> over Muram, which is a part of Russia. A king called
> Rodstaff ruled over a land called Rostov, and another
> king, Eddvald, ruled a kingdom called Suzdal. The
> king who ruled over Holmgard [i.e. Novgorod] before
> Quillanus was called Holmgeir. There was king called
> Paltes who ruled over Palteskja [i.e. Polostk]; and one
> called Kænmar ruled over Kænugard [i.e. Kiev] where
> the first settler had been Magog, the son of Japhet,
> Noah's son.

The names of the fictitious kings listed here are evidently
based on actual place names, just as King Siggeus in *YS*
got his name from the place Siggeum. Here we may quote
a brief account of Russia in a sober treatise on geography:
'In eastern Europe lies Gardariki [i.e. Russia]; located there
are Kænugard [Kiev], Holmgard [Novgorod] Palteskja
[Polotsk], and Smaleskja [Smolensk]. Next to Gardariki to
the south-west lies the kingdom of Greece; its principal city
is Constantinoplis, which we call Mikligard' (*Alfræði Islenzk
I*, p.110). Elsewhere we find a list of Russian rivers, including
the Dnjepr and the Dvina (*Hauksbók*, p.150). In the same
treatise on geography, a brief account of Russia follows the
section on Asia (p.155):

> In that part of the world is Europe; easternmost is
> Sweden the Great; that is where Philip the Apostle went
> to preach Christianity. In this region is the realm called
> Russia, which we call Gardariki; these are the princi-
> pal places there: Moramar [Muram], Rostofa [Rostov],
> Surdalar [Suzdal], Holmgard [Novgorod], Syrnes [?],
> Gadar [?], Palteskja [Polotsk], Kænugard [Kiev], of

which Magog, son of Japhet Noah's son, was the first inhabitant.

What is particularly striking about this list of Russian towns is that their names have Icelandic forms. 'Sweden the Great' is elsewhere in early Icelandic sources called 'Sweden the Cold'. But the true geographical sense of the term is made clear in various sources. Thus the Icelandic version of the life of Philip the Apostle tells us that he went to Scythia, 'which by some people is called "Sweden the Great".' The same identification Scythia with Sweden the Great, is made in *Alexanders Saga* and other Icelandic writings of the thirteenth century.

Scythia was located north and north-east of the Black Sea, so in terms of actual geography it corresponded to what is now South Russia. In a geographical treatise translated into Icelandic in the thirteenth century, we are told that 'Magon reigned over parts of Sweden the Great, but Madia over Kylfingaland, which we call Gardariki,' (*Hauksbók*, p. 164).[18] Here it is assumed the Kylfingaland/Gardariki forms a part of Scythia. In Snorri Sturluson's *Ynglinga Saga* (ch. 1) the Icelandic equivalent of Scythia denotes a vast country, extending all the way north into the Arctic regions:

> North of the Black Sea lies Sweden the Great or the Cold. People reckon that Sweden the Great is no smaller than Persia the Great, and some compare it to Ethiopia the Great. The northernmost part of 'Sweden' is uninhabitable because of the frost and the cold, just as the scorching sun renders desolate the southernmost part of Ethiopia. There are numerous large regions in 'Sweden'. Many different races are to be found there, and a good many separate languages. There are giants there, pygmies, black people, and all other kinds of exotic human beings. Also there are beasts and dragons of wondrously large size. From the mountains in the north which are situated beyond human habitation, a river properly named the Tanais [the old name for the River Don] flows through 'Sweden' . . . and into the Black Sea.

Snorri's ideas about Scythia are to a large extent based on foreign authorities, such as Isidore of Seville and other authors known to Odd Snorrason. In the grand design of *Ynglinga Saga*, Sweden the Great constitutes an important

27

part of the mythological map on which Snorri plots Odin's itinerary from Asia to Sweden proper. According to Snorri, who was following earlier authorities, the River Tanais [Don] separated not only Sweden the Great [Scythia] from Bactria, but also at the same time Europe from Asia. In other words, Sweden the Great lay in Asia, and a huge mountain range [the Caucasus] separated Scythia from other kingdoms. On Snorri's map, the two Swedens have alternative names, Sweden proper being labelled 'The World of Men' and Sweden the Great 'The World of Gods'. On his way to Sweden proper, Odin travels through Gardariki [Russia], which apparently lies west of Sweden the Great, and then to Saxony before reaching Scandinavia, his ultimate destination.

Although *YS* does not mention Scythia or Sweden the Great, Yngvar's odyssey takes him through strange regions which are reminiscent of various medieval descriptions of Scythia. It is a hopeless undertaking to try to identify the imaginary landscape and its inhabitants in *YS* with Russia, Georgia or any other part of what is now the Soviet Union. But we can compare Yngvar's discoveries to what it written about Scythia and other lands of the region in old books. Our concern is not so much to find out Yngvar's route to the east, as to identify the origin of the material that went into the imaginative description of that route. Odd Snorrason had evidently never been to Russia or the East. There is no likelihood that he ever visited Sweden the Great and absolutely no evidence that he had been to Sweden proper either. Odd strikes us as an armchair-traveller, the kind of person who takes a delight in guidebooks even though he never visits the foreign places he reads about. And since his oral informants must have been ignorant of the actual landscape, apart from the priest Isleif who had at least been to Sweden proper, he had to borrow ideas about Yngvar's discoveries from received authorities on geography.

Earlier we mentioned certain features in *YS* which came from learned books, and now we may briefly consider its particular affinities to early descriptions of Scythia. Individual features like the multiplication of languages, the presence of strange peoples and animals, including dragons, may not suffice to prove a connection between Isidore and *YS*, but when we add to these elements such a striking phenomena as a plenitude of gold and gems (cp. Isidore XIV. 3. 31), it seems highly unlikely that *YS* owes nothing to works such as those of Isidore and other medieval authorities. The wonders of the East were no doubt more clearly made manifest to the well-read Odd Snorrason than to the unfortunate Yngvar Eymundarson himself, in spite of all his travels.

v. Approaches to Russia

In a thirteenth-century note on pilgrim routes from Iceland, we are told that one could go on foot from Jutland, through Saxony, to Hungary and from there either east to Russia or else through Constantinople in Greece to Jerusalem. No Icelander or Scandinavian in medieval times is known to have taken that overland route to Russia, though it was the kind of itinerary that might have suited Brand the Far-Traveller and other devout Christians on a pilgrimage to Drofn near Polotsk to visit the grave of the widely-travelled missionary, Thorvald Kodransson. As we have seen, Thorvald himself approached Russia by a more usual route, travelling from Constantinople, across the Black Sea, and up the River Dnjepr. But most early Scandinavian visitors had more practical business in mind than the proselytising Thorvald and followed shorter and more northerly routes. First, those who were interested in the profitable fur trade would sail north along the west coast of Norway and Lapland, round the Kola Peninsula and across the White Sea to Permia. Second, from Sweden the Vikings could sail east across the Baltic, up the Gulf of Finland, into Lake Ladoga and so to Ladoga Town on the River Volkoz. From Ladoga Town it is only a short distance to Novgorod. Thirdly, the penetration into Russia could start farther south, from the coast of the Baltic States. Whichever course the Scandinavians chose, they could easily reach deep into the Ukraine (Kiev) or the heartland of Russia by river and portage, a method of travelling vividly remembered in *Yngvar's Saga*. Once on a south or south-east flowing major river, the traveller could sail to the Black Sea and Constantinople, or into the Caspian and to a market town in Persia. Certain Scandinavians may have gone to Russia in order 'to win fame and fortune' as Eymund is supposed to have done, but others certainly were essentially traders; to a third category belonged single-minded Vikings who offered nothing in return for what they took, but death and destruction. Finally, there were those who had tired of

Introduction

life in Sweden and decided to settle in the east. But visionary
explorers such as Yngvar the Far-Traveller, who fights his
way through hostile territories in search of the source of a
river, and tries to convert barbarous tribes to the Catholic
Faith, must have been rare birds among Scandinavians in
early Russia.

Our aim in this introduction is to attend to the details
of how Russia is presented in the Icelandic sagas, and avoid
the hazards created by speculative attempts to identify these
narrative events with the actual situation there in the Viking
period. Earlier we have considered references to Russia in
fictitious literature, and we shall have more to say below but
now we must take a brief look at the Kings' Sagas.[19] Several
of them describe Viking expeditions to Permia. As early as
the ninth century, the Norwegians had been trading with
the Permians. The earliest reference to such contacts is to
be found in King Alfred's Old English version of *Orosius*.[20]
Heimskringla states that Eirik Bloodaxe 'went north to
Finnmarken and all the way to Permia, where he fought
a great battle and won the day'. (I. p.135). *Egil's Saga*
describes Eirik's expedition in more detail: 'One spring he
made preparations for an expedition to Permia, taking every
care to fit things out properly . . . Eirik fought a great battle
in Permia on the River Dvina, and won the victory as poems
about him tell' (ch. 37). Later in *Heimskringla* (Saga of Olaf
Tryggvason ch. XIII) (I. p.217), Snorri Sturluson quotes a
tenth-century poet as evidence that one of Eirik's sons also
went to Permia:

> 'One summer Harald Grey-Cloak led his troops north
> to Permia and raided the country. He fought a great
> battle against the Permians on the banks of the River
> Dvina. He won the victory, killed many people, raided
> extensively in the land, and took a great deal of plunder.
> Glum Geirason mentions this:
>
>> In the east the outspoken
>> oppressor of princes
>> bloodied his burning
>> blade north of the burgh,
>> He made the Permians run
>> on this campaign, the peacemaker,
>> still a boy, fought a battle
>> on Dvina's banks.

30

Both these expeditions took place in the tenth century, and both were described by contemporary poets; evidently, Glum himself took part in the second expedition. The next Permia campaign mentioned in *Heimskringla* took place in 1026, and was led by Norwegian chieftains. As soon as they reached Permia, they started trading with the natives near the River Dvina and got a great deal of grey fur, beaver skins and sable. But after the trading was over, the Norwegians decided to make money by different means. Apparently it was a Permian custom that when a rich man died his money was divided between himself and his heirs. His share of the wealth was to be carried out into a forest, mixed with earth and buried in a mound. The same custom is described in *Arrow-Odd* (chs. 4–5). The Norwegians decided to rob such a mound, even though it was protected by the Permian god Jomali, and got away with a great deal of loot. Late in the eleventh century, King Hakon Magnusson (d.1094) is said to have 'gone north to Permia, fought a battle there, and won the victory.' In 1222 two Norwegian chieftains led a punitive expedition against the Permians, who had treacherously killed a number of Norwegians the year before, (*Hakon's Saga*, ch. 66). Sturla Thordarson who wrote the saga in 1265 adds that 'since then no trips have been made to Permia.'

The Kings' Sagas include several references to Ladoga Town and Novgorod, the two centres in Russia closest to Scandinavia. According to Snorri Sturluson's *Heimskringla*, Olaf Tryggvason was brought up in exile by King Valdimar of Russia, and in this respect Snorri agrees with Odd Snorrason's version of *Olaf Tryggvason's Saga*. But there are two significant differences between the accounts. Odd's *Olaf's Saga* does not say where King Valdimar resided, but Snorri, erroneously gives his residence as Novgorod, not Kiev. Secondly, Snorri tells us nothing about King Valdimar's conversion, while Odd Snorrason devotes the whole of his chapter 13 to it; according to Odd, Olaf has a dream in which the torments of Hell designed for heathen kings are revealed to him. As a result, Olaf goes to Greece, where truly wise Christians tell him of Christ and he receives provisional baptism. Wishing to save his foster-father King Valdimar from this terrible fate,

   . . .Olaf went back to Russia and was given a good welcome. He stayed there a while saying to the king and queen that they should do what was best for them, and that it was a much fairer thing to believe in the true God our Creator who made heaven and earth and all things that belong to them. He also told them that it was not good for men of power to lose their way in such great darkness that they have faith in a god who can give them no help, devoting all their time and effort to this.

'You must also understand wisely that what we tell you is true. I shall never cease to teach you the true faith or the word of God, so that you may offer to him the fruit of your being.'

Although the king resisted a long time, rejecting the idea of giving up his beliefs and the worship of his gods, yet through God's mercy he was able to understand that there was a vast difference between the faith he held to and the one preached by Olaf. He was also often eloquently reminded that what he had practised was idolatry and superstition whereas Christians had a better and more beautiful faith. And with the wholesome counsel of the queen which she offered to this end and with the aid and mercy of God the king agreed and all his men to accept Holy Baptism and the true Faith, and all the people there became Christians. (*Olaf Tryggvason's Saga*, ch. 13).

In 1988 there were celebrations of 1000 years of Christianity in Russia, following the conversion of King Valdimar. We do not know how much attention was paid to the efforts of Olaf. Odd almost certainly had his information from some written source, but unfortunately this story cannot be reconciled with the known facts of the life of King Olaf.

As we have mentioned, Olaf probably took charge of Russia's defences at the age of eighteen – the conventional age for a saga hero to take such responsibilities – and was nineteen years' old when he left Russia. Snorri gives a brief description of a viking expedition into Russia towards the end of the tenth century:

In the autumn Earl Eirik sailed back to Sweden and spent another winter there. And in the spring the earl made his ships ready and sailed to the east. As soon as he arrived in Valdimar's kingdom, he started slaughtering the inhabitants and burning everything wherever he came, laying the land waste. He came to Ladoga Town, and laid siege to it until he captured the town, killing a good many people, demolishing the town and burning it to the ground. Afterwards he plundered Russia far and wide. This is what is said in *Bandadrápa*:

In the war-storm of weapons
the wealthy one laid waste
Valdimar's soil, sacked
Ladoga Town, scourge of men.
True what we were told,
the battle was tough there,
when you reached the realm
of the Russians.[21]

Earl Eirik was not the only Norwegian in his lifetime to lead a viking expedition to Russia. His half-brother Earl Svein 'brought his troops east to Russia, plundering there. He stayed there over the summer, but in the autumn he returned to Sweden' (*Heimskringla II, 71*). This is supposed to have taken place *c.*1015. Here, as so often in the sagas, the author appears to be ignorant of the precise location of events in Russia. But when our sources are contemporary verse the situation becomes clearer, as is the case of the stanza above where Ladoga Town is specifically mentioned.

Notwithstanding viking raids in Russia, some of its rulers enjoyed a special relationship with Scandinavian royalty. Two of Norway's kings were brought up in Russia, Olaf Tryggvason by King Valdimar (see above, p.12; 31), and Magnus the Good by King Jarisleif. Important for this special relationship was the marriage of Jarisleif and Ingigerd (see above, p.10; 46), which meant that the ruler of Russia became son-in-law to the King of Sweden, brother-in-law to the Queen of Norway. In such circumstances it is not surprising that King Olaf the Saint should seek refuge with King Jarisleif and entrust him with the task of bringing up his son Magnus. (See *Heimskringla; Flateyjarbók*.) After the battle of Stiklarstad (1030), where King Olaf the Saint met his death, his brother Harald travelled east to Russia and spent several years there. In accordance with narrative convention King Jarisleif gave Harald the role of 'young defender', (see above, p.13). In due course Harald sailed to Constantinople, where he spent a number of years in the service of the Emperor. Many adventures later, Harald made his way back from Byzantium across the Black Sea to a place called 'Ellipalter' which has been identified as the estuary of the River Dnjepr. In Russia, Harald married Princess Elizabeth, King Jarisleif's daughter. In Norse her name was given a new form Ellisif, where the second element appears to be the name of Thor's wife in mythology (Sif). It has been suggested that the name ('Silkisif') in *Yngvar's Saga* and *Arrow-Odd* was modelled on 'Ellisif'.[22]

The wedding took place in the winter. 'In the spring he set out from Novgorod, travelling from there to Ladoga Town, where he got a ship, and sailed that summer west to Sweden.' (*Heimskringla III*, 91). Magnus the Good took the same route: 'After Christmas Magnus Olafsson began his journey from the east from Novgorod to Ladoga Town, where he fitted out his ships as soon as the ice broke in the spring.' There are still several stanzas extant alluding to Harald's stay in Russia, but there is nothing further of significance to report about his dealings with Russia, for after becoming King of Norway he turned his mind to the west, and died on a military campaign in Yorkshire on a hot sunny day, 21 September, 1066. King Sigurd the Crusader (d.1130) married 'Malmfrid, the daughter of King Harald Valdimarsson of Novgorod in the east,' (*Heimskringla III*, 258). The importance of the blood relationship between the royal families of Norway and Russia lingered on for a long time. (Cp. *Heimskringla III*.) The royal families of Denmark and Russia were also linked. (See *Knytlinga Saga*, chs. 11, 88). One of the Danish princes in the twelfth century, Valdimar Knutsson (d.1182) was Russian on his mother's side, as his name suggests, and brought up in Russia. (ch. 93). Following a poem by Markus Skeggjason (d.1107), *Knytlinga Saga* (ch. 70) describes a journey by Eirik Sveinsson (later king of Denmark, d.1103) 'all the way east to Russia, visiting the homes of chieftains and other great men, all of whom welcomed him with friendship and respect, and received fine gifts from powerful leaders.'

As we saw earlier, the year 1222 marks the end of Norwegian attacks upon the long-suffering Permians, who were threatened from other quarters as well. In a long list of undated 'good deeds' by King Hakon of Norway (d.1263), Sturla Thórdarson includes the following item: 'A good many Permians came to him who had fled to the west because the Tartars attacked them. He converted them to Christianity and gave them the fjord that is called Malangen.' (*Hakon's Saga*, ch. 338). The Icelanders and the Greenlanders had no reason to love King Hakon who had forced them to surrender their precious independence, but credit must be given where due. King Hakon knew how to make refugees from the east feel at home in the west: not only did he give them land to settle (the fjord Malangen in the north of Norway), he showed them the error of their ways by putting an end to their allegiance to their noble god, Jomali.

Hakon's Saga (ch. 238) includes an interesting account of diplomatic activity between Russia and Norway:

'This winter [i.e. 1250–51] which King Hakon spent in Trondheim, the envoys of King Alexander of Novgorod came west from Russia. Their leader, a knight, was called Michael. They made protests about what happened when King Hakon's sheriffs in Finnmarken clashed with the East-Karelians, who were tributary to the king of Novgorod, for each side kept robbing and killing the other. Meetings were arranged to deal with the matter, and it was decided how to settle the issue. The envoys had another mission: they wanted to meet King Hakon's daughter, Lady Kristina, because the king of Novgorod had commanded them to find out if King Hakon would be willing to give the lady in marriage to his son. What King Hakon did was to dispatch his own messengers in the spring with King Alexander's envoys from Trondheim east to Novgorod. In charge of the Norwegian mission were Vigleik the Priests's-son and Borgar. They travelled first to Bergen and then followed the eastern route, arriving in Novgorod in the summer. The king gave them a good welcome, and agreed on peace terms between themselves and their tributary lands, that neither the Lapps nor the Karelians should show any hostility to the other. But that settlement did not last long. At that time there was a bitter war going on in Novgorod, with the Tartars constantly attacking the kingdom, which is why the marriage proposal he had suggested was not given due consideration. When they had finished their business, the Norwegians went back west, laden with splendid gifts which the king of Novgorod had sent to King Hakon, and arrived back home in the winter and met the king at Oslo.'

Introduction

About the same time, we find a distinguished Russian in the company of Earl Birgir of Sweden: 'Also present there was King Andrew of Suzdal, the brother of King Alexander of Novgorod.' (*Hakon's Saga*, ch. 245).

Turning from the historical records, we move again into the world of fiction. Descriptions of Permia in *The History of the Danes* by Saxo Grammaticus (d.1216) depict it as a singularly cold and inhospitable country, whose inhabitants are given to sorcery and witchcraft. And in the Icelandic accounts, the Permians appear as a hostile tribe. The title hero of *Arrow-Odd* moves with ease from Norway to Permia and back home again. His encounter with the Permians is reminiscent of what we read about them in the Kings' Sagas. After excursions to Sweden, Ireland, England, France and other more or less civilised countries in Europe, Arrow-Odd finds himself first in mythical Giantland and later in Slabland, an Arctic waste on the far side of the Atlantic. A good many adventures later he becomes the king of Greece, and it is from there that he sets out to destroy his elusive and invincible enemy, King Quillanus of Novgorod. The blood-brothers in *Bosi and Herraud* belong to Scandinavia and make several excursions to Permia, whose ruler has connections with King Godmund of the imaginary Siberian wasteland, Glasis Plains, mentioned above (p.18). (References to the Permian god Jomali suggests that the author may have been familiar with the *Saga of King Olaf the Saint*.) The father of the title hero of *Halfdan Eysteinsson* is the son of a provincial king in Norway. King Eystein leads a military expedition to Russia, kills the ruler of Ladoga Town, usurps his kingdom and marries the widow, but is himself later killed in revenge. His son Halfdan inherits the difficult task of avenging his father in a hostile land. In the final and decisive battle, Halfdan comes face to face with King Harek of Permia, who figures in other tales besides this one. Conveniently, Harek transforms himself into a dragon. But everything turns out well in the end, and after memorable victories in Permia and beyond, Halfdan goes back to his ancestral kingdom in Norway.

Earlier in this Introduction we referred to *Egil and Asmund*, who travel from Scandinavia to Russia where they take on the role of 'the young defender'. From there they set out in search of a pair of princesses who have been abducted

36

to the mythical Jotunheim. In their quest, Egil and Asmund are given aid by a giantess who had slept with Thor himself and visited the mysterious Underworld. Like certain other Viking romances, the tale ends happily with the completion of the quest and wedding-bells for the principal characters.

Göngu-Hrolf's Saga figures the likeable King Hreggvid of Novgorod, killed at the beginning of the tale, which deals with the recovery of the kingdom for his daughter. One of the less pleasant members of the cast is:

> A great and powerful king called Menelaus who ruled over the land of Tartary, believed to be the largest country and the richest in gold throughout the entire Orient. The folk there are big and strong, and the hardest of fighting men. Many tributary kings served under Menelaus, as well as other important chieftains. It is said that an island lies between Russia and Tartary called Hedin's Isle, an earldom . . .

The geography here appears somewhat eccentric; the author may have borrowed the notion of Tartary from *Hakon's Saga*, describing the dealings of the king of Novgorod with the Tartars (see above, p.35). The name Menelaus probably comes from *Trojumanna Saga*, and Hedin's Isle echoes the tragic tale of Hedin and Hogni. Such is the eclectic nature of these stories, and the similarity of many of their features to the two tales in this volume, that they reinforce our doubts about some of the scholarly attempts to locate our tales precisely in Russian history and geography. In *Gautrek's Saga* there is a reference to King Sisar of Kiev, who is just as unhistorical as Kings Yngvar (in *Sturlaug's Saga*), and Hergeir of Ladoga Town, and King Eirik and Earl Ottar of Novgorod elsewhere in the fictive literature. In *Half's Saga* we find King Hjorleif of Hordaland sailing up to the River Dvina in Permia, fighting the natives, breaking into a burial mound, and coming away with a great deal of loot. *Sturlaug's Saga* describes a pagan temple west of the River Dvina, but here there is no sign of the noble Permian god Jomali, only Thor and other commonplace gods from Norse mythology.

The contrast between 'Sweden proper, the world of Men' and 'Sweden the Great, the World of Gods', alluded to above, serves to remind us of the ambivalent situation of Russia in early Icelandic literature as a whole. While certain oft-mentioned places in Russia, such as Ladoga Town, Novgorod, and Kiev, were recognised as integral parts of the rational map of the world, the fictional literature suggested that not so far beyond them were purely mythical regions, inhabited by dragons and monsters, such as those of *Yngvar's Saga*. As we pointed out earlier, Odin is supposed to have come from Asia, and by a slick piece of medieval etymology the name of the continent because associated with the word *ás*-one of the Norse terms for a pagan god. This is how Snorri Sturluson puts it in *Ynglinga Saga*: 'The country east of the River Tanais is in *Asia* and was called *Asaland* or *Asaheim*, but the principal place in the land they called *Asgard*,' (ch. 2). So when the hero of a fictitious tale reaches Russia, he may travel beyond it and soon find himself in a purely imaginary landscape. The name *Asgard*, one of the best known locations in the world of Norse myth, is interesting here not only because of its first element, but also because the second part of the compound was bound to remind the reader of other city names in the east compounded in *-gard:* (in the sense of 'town') *Mikligard* (Constantinople), *Kænugard* (Kiev), *Holmgard* (Novgorod); nor should it be forgotten that the most common names for Russia in Icelandic were *Gardar* and *Gardariki*.

In view of this situation, it is not surprising to find in *Göngu-Hrolf's Saga* that Giantland lies within travelling distance of Russia, or that the mythical Glasis Plains in *Bosi and Herraud* belongs to the same map. It is this quality of Russia that we must bear in mind when we try to make sense of Yngvar's journey, terminable only with his death, to the source of a Russian river which must lie far east of Russia itself, somewhere in Asialand.

Notes

1 Larsson (1987) argues that 'the saga (*YS*) includes parts which definitely can be stated to have a realistic core' (p.106). He cites the description of Greek fire (*YS*, ch. 6) and 'the account of the round boats which seem to be very similar to the quffas of Eufrat and Tigris' (*YS*, ch. 5) and where the saga describes the Red Sea, Larsson argues 'a very close correspondence between that description and the real conditions at Kara-Bugaz (The Black Abyss) by the Eastern Caspian sea . . . the salt bay, into

Introduction

which this rapid falls, lights the sky with a red tone, according
to Russian descriptions' (p.107). We feel less confident about
such exact identifications, though the references to some native
practices such as the bearing of feathers and the wearing of a
bird's-head mask, or the three magic apples (*YS*, ch. 9) may be
echoes of Shaman customs amongst the tribes of Asiatic Russia:
see Mircea Eliade, *Shamanism* (London, 1964), pp.78; 156–7.

2 Like the two other great centres of learning in the south of
Iceland, Haukadal and Skalholt, Oddi was far less isolated
from European culture than a casual saga reader might think.
Sæmund the Learned was educated in France and his return to
Iceland as a mature scholar at the age of twenty was considered
important enough to merit a mention in the meagre *Icelandic
Annals* (s.a. 1076). Thorlak Thorhallsson (1133–1193) was
brought up at Oddi and later completed his studies in Paris
and Lincoln. He was the first Head of the Augustinian House
at Thykkvbær in Ver (1168–75) and later bishop of Skalholt
(1178–93). His nephew and successor as bishop, Páll Jonsson,
son of Jón Loftsson, also received his basic education at Oddi and
studied later at Lincoln. 'He went to England and was at school
there, where it is said he acquired so much learning that there has
probably never been anyone who learnt as much over an equal
period. When he came back to Iceland he surpassed all other
men in the refinement of his knowledge, versification and book
learning.' (*The Saga of Bishop Páll*, p.128). Another interesting
fact about Oddi in the second half of the twelfth century was its
close links with Orkney; on his way to England, Páll spent some
time with Earl Harald at Kirkwall.

3 The principal sources about Gizur Hallsson are *Hungurvaka*, *The
Saga of Bishop Thorlak*, *The Saga of Bishop Páll* and *Sturlunga
saga*. Gizur's father Hall Teitsson (1085–1150), was such an
exceptional linguist that he was said to speak every language
between Iceland and Rome like a native. (Cp. *Hungurvaka*, p.
80). It has been suggested that Hall is the author of *The First
Grammatical Treatise*, apparently written about the middle of the
twelfth century, by someone with remarkable linguistic skills.

4 *Flateyjarbók 1* (1944), p.575. The same source lists six narrators, three men and three women, who provided Gunnlaug
Leifsson and Odd Snorrason with oral information about King
Olaf Tryggvason (d.AD 1000). When Gunnlaug and Odd were
gathering materials for their books on King Olaf late in the
twelfth century, there were very few written sources available
to them.

5 *Isidori Hispalensis Episcopi Etymologiarum Sive Originum Libri
XX*. Ed. W.M. Lindsay (Oxford, 1911) XV.1,33: 'Heliopolis
urbs Aegypti, quae Latine interpretatur solis civitas.' Heliopolis

is a town in Egypt, which in Latin means 'The City of the Sun'. Here we might quote from Shepard's erudite article (p.278): 'Larsson proposes to identify Citopolis with the capital of western Gerogia, Kutaisi (classical Cytaea). Such an identification is tempting, but incurs the objection that the name could equally well reflect a story-teller's pretensions to scholarship (Citopolis < Scythopolis), as do the names of Hieliopolis/Hieriopolis and Siggeum . . . Larsson himself concedes that the promontary Siggeum has been confused with the Sigeum of the Hellespont.' See also Olson *YS* pp.lxxxi and lxxxv; Larsson, p.100; Hofmann, p.208.

6 Isidore, XIV. 7.2: 'Sigeum promuntorium Asiae, ubi Hellespontus apertius dilatatur . . .' Sigeum is a promontary in Asia where the Hellespont becomes wider.' The name Siggeum also occurs in *Trójumanna saga*, the medieval Icelandic version of the Troy Legend.

7 Isidore, XI. 3.16: 'Cyclopes. quoque eadem India gignit; et dictos Cyclopes eo quod unum habere oculum in fronte media perhibentur. Hi et agriophagitai dicuntur, propter quod solas ferarum carnes edunt': 'Likewise, India also brings forth the Cyclopes; they are called the Cyclopes because they are said to have one eye in the middle of the forehead. They are also called *agriophatigai*, because they eat only the flesh of wild animals'. A Norse version of the Latin paragraph is to be found in *Stjórn*, a medieval Norse version of parts of the Old Testament, including some exegetical material pp.78–9). In *Hauksbók* (p.166) it is stated that 'Cyclopes' have a single eye in the middle of the forehead.

8 XII 4, 29: 'Iaculus serpens volens': The Jaculus is a flying dragon.

9 Cp. Isidore IX2, 132; *Hauksbók*, p.165.

10 *Göngu-Hrolf's Saga*, pp.28–9, where note 1 on page 29 contains misleading information regarding the dating of *YS*. It should also be noted that the so-called *Konungsannáll* dates Yngvar's death to AD 1041, which agrees with *YS*. But there is a textual problem here. Whereas the MS reading we have followed stated that Yngvar died *eleven* years after the fall of King Olaf Haraldsson the Saint, another MS has *nine*. King Olaf was killed in 1030, and his death is used elsewhere for such dating purposes, e.g. Ari the Learned's *Life of Snorri the Priest:* 'Snorri the Priest . . . died one year after the fall of King Olaf the Saint' (*Islenzk fornrit IV*, p.186; this statement is repeated in both *Laxdæla Saga* and *Eybryggja Saga*). In the *Saga of Bishop Jón* we are told that Jón was born twenty-two years after the fall of King Olaf the Saint. (ch. 1). In its present form, excluding additional matter, *Konungsannáll* appears to belong to the end of

Introduction

the thirteenth century. However it was probably based on earlier
annalistic notes. There can be little doubt about its provenance:
internal evidence suggests it was compiled in the Benedictine
monastery of Thingeyrar, where the Latin original of *YS* was
written almost a century earlier. It has been pointed out that a
good many entries in the annal for the period 1151–1237 concern the family of a certain farmer who retired to the monastery
shortly after the middle of the thirteenth century. (See H.P.
1965, pp.50–51; and 1970, pp.39–43). Here, as elsewhere,
Lögmannsannáll (to the year 1362) which was written by Einar
Haflidason in the vicinity of Thingeyrar, follows *Konungsannáll*
closely and has therefore no independent value. The problem of
dating is discussed in some detail by Shepard, pp.255–8, with
reference to previous scholars.

11 Cp. Robert Cook's remark about *YS*: 'No one would imagine
that there was any truth to this highly fanciful account of the
adventures of a party of Swedes in Russia, were it not that some
twenty-six runic stones in the Malar region testify that an Yngvar
actually led an expedition into the East' (67).

12 For the runic texts see Olson, pp.51–65; and *Sveriges
runinskrifter III* (1924–1936). The following examples may serve
to indicate the nature and purpose of these inscriptions. 'Þjalfi
and Holmlaug had all these stones erected in the memory of
their son Banki, who owned a ship which he captained east in
Yngvar's army. May God save Banki's soul. Askel carved (this
stone).

Geirve and Gylla erected this stone in memory of their father
Onund, who met his death in the east with Yngvar. May God
help their souls.

Andvit and Kar and Gisli and Blesi and Djarf erected this
stone in memory of their father Gunnleif, who was killed in the
east with Yngvar. May God help their souls. I, Alrik carved the
runes. He was good at steering the ship.

Herleif and Thorgerd had this stone erected in memory of
their father Sæbjorn who captained a ship with Yngvar east to
Estonia.

Klint and Bleik erected this stone in memory of their father
Gunnvid. He went away with Yngvar. God the Lord save the
souls of all Christians. Thorir trana carved (the runes).

Gunnulf erected this stone in memory of his father Ulf. He
travelled east with Yngvar.

Tola had this stone erected in memory of her son Harald,
Yngvar's brother. They travelled boldly far away for gold, and
in the east they fed the eagle. They died in south in Serkland.

Andvit erected the stone in memory of his brother Haugi, who
met his death with Yngvar; also in memory of his good brother

41

Thorgils. Bjarnlaug, the heir, had the stone erected in memory of his father.' (Translation based on Olson's edition, *Yngvar's Saga*, pp.51–65).

13 In addition to the three Russian brothers, attention may be drawn to the following triads: Eymund has two brothers, Hrærek and Dag, and two blood-brothers, King Olaf and Ragnar Agnarsson; three battles are fought with Burislaf; three sisters, Asta, Thorny, and Isrid, are mentioned in ch. 1; the tripartite division of Russian into Kiev, Novgorod and Polotsk.

14 Discussing the historical record of the period of independence of the Polyane in his article 'From the Varangians to the Greeks and other matters', Professor Ward favours 'the time before the arrival of the Varangians in Kiev' and renders the following passage from the Russian *Chronicle:*

At the time when the Polyane were still leading an independent tribal existence in the hills around Kiev there was a (known) sea-route from the Baltic to the Byzantine world. One could also travel from the Byzantine world up the Dnieper, thence by portage across to the Lovat' and along this river to Lake Il´men´. Lake Il´men´ is joined by the river Volkhov to Lake Ladoga, which in turn is connected with the Baltic by the river Neva. The sea-route then leads to Rome, thence to Constantinople, from where one can sail further, into the Black Sea, into which the Dnieper flows. Now the Dnieper rises in the Okov Forest (in the heart of Rus') and flows south, whereas the Dvina and Volga, which both rise in the same forest, flow respectively north into the Baltic and east into the Caspian. Thus one can travel from Rus' down the Volga to the land of the Bulgars and then further, across the Caspian, to Khwarezmia and the Orient; down the Dvina to the Baltic, thence to Rome and, from Rome, to Africa; and down the Dnieper to the Black Sea, on the south coast of which, so the story goes, St Andrew, Peter's brother, once preached. See bibliography, Dennis Ward.

15 See Walter Scott, 'Abstract of the *Eyrbyggja Saga*' in M. Mallet (ed.), *Illustrations of Northern Antiquities* (1814).

16 Seven Viking Romances, Harmondsworth, 1985 pp.9–14. See also Paul Edwards, "Ambiguous Seductions: 'La Belle Dame Sans Merci', 'The Faerie Queene', and 'Thomas the Rhymer' ", in *Durham University Journal*, forthcoming 1989.

17 See the introduction to *Magnus' Saga: The Life of St Magnus, Earl of Orkney 1075–1116* (Oxford, 1987).

18 As far as we know, this is the only reference to Kylfingaland in early Icelandic sources, but *Egil's Saga* (ch. 10) mentions the tribal name *Kylfingar* in connection with Thorolf's expedition to Finnmark: 'When he reached the mountains to the east he learned that the Kylfing tribe had travelled west to trade with

Introduction

the Lapps and pick up some loot on the side. Thorolf appointed several Lapps to keep an eye open for the Kylfings' movements, and set out himself in search of them. At one place he came upon a group of about thirty Kylfings and killed the lot. Not one of them got away.' Several attempts have been made to identify the *Kylfingar*, most recently by Shepard (p.227) as the equivalent of Russian *Kolbyag*. 'The term Kylfing (*Kolbyag*) seems to have designated traders of North Germanic origin . . .'

19 The Sagas of the Icelanders have very little to say about Russia, and what they say is of scant historical value. Earlier we mentioned *Bjorn's Saga*, whose hero saves Valdimar's kingdom by killing a potential usurper of the throne. Needless to say, Russian sources offer no corroborative evidence for Bjorn's valiant exploits. *Egil's Saga* and *Kormak's Saga*, however, mention events associated with Russia which are described in the Kings' Saga, which were probably their sources. *Heidarvíga Saga* tells how the principal character, Bardi, went to Russia where he joined the Varangians; elsewhere in early Icelandic sources the Varangians are exclusively associated with Constantinople and the Eastern Empire. This detail in *Heidarviga Saga* may be based on genuine oral tradition. In *Njál's Saga*, 'Kolskegg was baptized in Denmark. But he never found happiness there, and moved on east to Russia, where he stayed for one winter. From there he travelled to Constantinople, where he joined the Emperor's army. The last that was heard of him was that he married there and became a leader in the Varangian Guard (ch. 81). Elsewhere in *Njál's Saga*, a Norwegian claims to have sailed 'to every land between Norway and Russia, and even as far as Permia.' (ch. 28).

20 See Alan S.C. Ross, *The Terfinnas and Beormas of Ohtere* (London, 1981).

21 *Heimskringla I*. 338–9. *Bandadrápa* was composed by a contemporary poet called Eyjolf the Deed-Scald and is therefore a reliable source.

22 As scholars have pointed out, the three names *Ellisif, Silkisif,* and *Hildisif* are probably all late formations. As a matter of curiosity we mention that in scaldic verse the name 'Sif' figures in several kennings for women, such as *Hirdi-Sif, Hristi-Sif, Reidi-Sif*. See Finnur Jónsson, *Lexicon Poeticum* (Cop. 1931), pp.492–3.

YNGVAR'S SAGA

1. King Eirik and his family

A king called Eirik ruled over Sweden: he was called Eirik the Conqueror. He married Sigrid the Haughty, but since she was a hard woman to live with, overbearing in everything she did, he divorced her – though he let her have Gotaland. Their son was Olaf the Swede.

This happened when Earl Hakon was ruler of Norway: he had a good many children and we shall have more to say about one of his daughters, Aud.

King Eirik had a daughter whose name is not known, and a Swedish chieftain called Aki wanted to marry her, but since he was not well-born the king thought him unacceptable. Shortly after that, a provincial king from Russia asked for her, and King Eirik was in favour of his marriage to the girl, so she travelled back with him to Russia. A little later, Aki turned up unexpectedly, killed the king and carried the princess back to Sweden, where he made her his wife. There were eight other chieftains involved in this plot with Aki, and for some time they had to bear with Eirik's hostility, although he didn't want to fight them and risk heavy loss of life amongst the people of his own kingdom. Aki and the princess had a son who was called Eymund.

Some time after, Aki sought reconciliation with King Eirik for his reckless behaviour and the King seemed agreeable: at that time he was proposing marriage with Aud, the daughter of Earl Hakon of Norway. His approaches were favourably received, but the earl made it known that it would please him if King Eirik's self-appointed son-in-law were to have his royal privileges in Sweden withdrawn. Pledges were sworn and a day was fixed for the wedding.

44

There were new exchanges between Aki and King Eirik, and it was agreed that Aki would abide by any terms decided by the king as long as he did not have to go into exile: so they were reconciled. Now the king started preparations for his wedding feast, inviting chieftains from all over the kingdom, and the first people he asked were his son-in-law Aki and the eight chieftains in league with him.

2. The Death of Aki

Earl Hakon of Norway arrived at Uppsala in Sweden on the appointed day. A great assembly of people had gathered including all the most important men in the land. A number of great halls had been built to accommodate the many chieftains who were coming with their whole retinues. After King Eirik and Earl Hakon, Aki was the one with the biggest following, so he was given the second largest hall, but the king's daughter and her son stayed away as there seemed to be something suspicious about the invitation.

The wedding guests now began to enjoy themselves and there was a great deal of mirth and merrymaking. At first Aki was on his guard but after the celebrations had been going on for some time he grew less wary. On the last day of the festivities, King Eirik came and took all of them by surprise, killing Aki and his eight fellow-plotters who had rebelled against royal authority. After that the wedding feast came to an end, Earl Hakon went back to Norway, and each guest to his own home. Some people say that Earl Hakon thought up this scheme, some that he himself took part in the killing.

Now King Eirik laid claim to possession of all the estates and property owned by the eight chieftains. He took Eymund and the boy's mother home with him, and Eymund grew up with the king in high favour until Eirik's death, after which King Olaf took charge of the state, treating Eymund with the same respect Eymund had received from Olaf's father, King Eirik.

But as Eymund grew older he began to think about his grievances, for he could see daily, before his very eyes, the possessions which were properly his. He felt he had been cheated out of his birthright, since the king collected all the dues from his estates, King Olaf had a daughter called Ingigerd, in every way a most accomplished young woman, and she and her cousin Eymund were very much in love. Eymund was a tall, powerfully-built man and the best of knights.

So Eymund kept brooding over his troubles. It seemed to him pointless to sit waiting for compensation for his wrongs: better for a quick death, he thought, than a life a shame. One day he discovered that the king had sent out twelve of his retainers to collect tribute from the estates that had once belonged to Eymund's father, so he set off with a dozen companions and ambushed the king's men in a forest. There he set on them, and a fierce fight began.

On that same day, Ingigerd happened to be travelling through the forest and found all of them dead, apart from Eymund who was badly wounded. She laid him down in her cart, drove him home and healed him in secret. But when King Olaf heard the news, he summoned people to a formal meeting, and declared Eymund an outlaw throughout his kingdom. When Eymund recovered, Ingigerd provided him secretly with a ship to sail on a viking expedition. He had good men, and there were rich pickings.

3. Reconciliation

Some years later, a king called Jarisleif who ruled over Russia proposed to Ingigerd, married her, and took her back east. When Eymund heard the news he travelled to Russia in order to visit them, and both Jarisleif and Ingigerd welcomed him warmly. At that time Russia was in a state of war, for Burislaf, King Jarisleif's brother, was making attacks on the kingdom. Eymund fought against him in five battles, and in the last battle Burislaf was captured, blinded, and brought before the king. Eymund won a great deal in the way of plunder – gold, silver, and all kinds of treasures and valuable possessions.

Ingigerd sent messengers to her father, King Olaf, asking him to give up the estates that belonged to Eymund, since it would be better for him to be reconciled to Eymund than live in fear of an armed attack. To all appearances, Olaf went along with this.

Meanwhile, Eymund was in Novgorod fighting many a battle, always gaining the victory, and recovering for the king many of his tributary territories. But then Eymund began to long to go home and visit his estates. With a large, well-equipped force of men and plenty of money and weapons, he set out from Russia with the respect and admiration of all, and came back to Sweden, where he took charge of his estates and whatever else he owned. Soon afterwards he began looking for a wife, and married the daughter of a landed man, having a son by her called Yngvar.

King Olaf of Sweden was told that Eymund had come ashore with a large force and a great deal of money, and had taken charge of the estates that his father and the other eight chieftains had once owned. Olaf was very much put out by this, but felt there was nothing he could do about it, for every day he heard about Eymund's heroic exploits: and since neither was willing to give way, they left each other in peace.

Now Eymund settled down to rule and run his estates as if he were a king. As he added to his territories, so his subjects grew in number. He had a palatial hall built for himself, lavishly furnished, and feasted many guests there daily, for he had a large body of knights and a well-manned fleet: and there, in peace and quiet, he settled down.

Yngvar grew up with his father. When he was nine years' old, he asked his father's permission to visit King Olaf and other leading men in Sweden. Eymund allowed him to go and fitted him out handsomely. Yngvar took his father's finest gilt helmet, set with precious stones, a gold-adorned sword, and many other precious possessions. Then he set out from his father's hall with fourteen men, each one in armour, bearing a shield, and riding armoured horses. They wore gilded helmets and all their weapons were embellished with silver and gold. Yngvar travelled with this force east through Sweden and his journey was spoken of far and wide: everywhere he went, chieftains came to meet him and invite him to feast with them, and all these invitations he accepted, exchanging valuable gifts.

Yngvar's fame spread to all parts of Sweden and reached the ears of King Olaf. Olaf had a son called Onund, a promising youngster about the same age as Yngvar. Onund asked his father to let him go and meet his cousin Yngvar to give him a proper welcome, and the king gave his permission. So he set out in fine style to meet Yngvar and they greeted one another with great affection. Together they went to see the king, who came out to meet them and gave them a friendly

47

welcome. He led Yngvar into his great hall, set him next to himself, and invited him to stay there with all his men for as long as he wished. Yngvar said he would stay for a while.

Then Yngvar showed the precious things we spoke of, the helmet and the sword.

'My father sends you these gifts,' he said, 'to seal the friendship and peace between you.'

The king received the gifts graciously, but remarked that it could not have been Eymund who sent them.

Yngvar spent the whole winter there and the king held him in higher respect than any other man. In the spring, Yngvar made preparations to return home and Onund decided to go with him. The king gave Yngvar a fine horse, a gilded saddle and a handsome ship, and saw Yngvar and Onund off in style on their journey to Eymund.

When they came to Eymund's residence he was told they had arrived but pretended not to have heard. Onund wanted to dismount outside the great hall but Yngvar said they should ride straight inside and that is what they did, right up to Eymund's high-seat. He gave them a friendly greeting and asked the news, but enquired why they had been so bold as to ride roughshod into his hall.

'When I went to visit King Olaf,' said Yngvar, 'he came outside with all his retainers to greet me and give me an honourable welcome: but when his son pays you a visit you show him no respect, and I want you to know it was for that reason I came riding into your hall.'

At that, Eymund sprang to his feet, helped Onund from the saddle with his own hands, embraced him and set him down, saying that everyone at court would be at his service. Then Yngvar gave his father the gifts, telling him King Olaf had sent the horse, the saddle and the ship to confirm the peace between them. Eymund praised King Olaf for having presented such gifts to Yngvar, but said he could not believe that the gifts were intended for himself.

Onund stayed with them over winter and in the spring he made ready to leave for home. Yngvar travelled with him. Eymund gave Onund a gold-feathered hawk, and so they set out on their way until they came back to King Olaf, who was delighted to see them and gave them a great welcome. Onund presented him with the hawk and said this was a gift Eymund had sent him.

The king flushed red, and said that perhaps Eymund might have mentioned his name when he made a gift of the hawk – 'so maybe he had me in mind'.

'Now you must go back to Eymund,' he said, 'and give him this banner from me: there's no gift I could send him more precious. It has this magic quality, that whoever has it carried before him is bound to be victorious. Let it seal the peace between us.'

They travelled back to Eymund and gave him the banner, telling him what the king had said. Eymund received the royal gift with pleasure and told them to hurry back with an invitation to King Olaf. This is what they were to say to him: 'Your servant Eymund cordially invites you to a feast and would be deeply grateful if you would come.'

When they returned to King Olaf and gave him the message from Eymund, he was delighted and set off with a large following. Eymund greeted him warmly and with great respect, and they agreed to become close friends, an agreement they kept.

Later, King Olaf travelled home laden with splendid gifts. Yngvar stayed with him most of the time, for the king loved him no less than his own son. Yngvar was a tall, handsome man, strong and fair-complexioned. He was shrewd and well-spoken, kind and generous to his friends, ruthless to his enemies, a courteous man and always correct in his conduct: as a result, wise men have often compared him to his kinsman Styrbjorn, and to King Olaf Tryggvason, the most famous in the eyes of God and men ever to have come out of Scandinavia, or who ever will, to the end of time.

4. *In the King's Service*

It so happened that when the cousins Onund and Yngvar were grown men, a people called the Semgalls rebelled against King Olaf and for some time paid him no tribute, so King Olaf sent Onund and Yngvar with three ships to collect it. They came to the land of the Semgalls, summoned them to a meeting, and ordered their king to pay up. Yngvar then showed what an accomplished speaker he was, for he persuaded the king and most of his chieftains that there was nothing for it but to pay the tribute to which he was laying claim. But there were three chieftains who would not follow their king's advice, and they refused to pay the tax. They

gathered their forces, but when the king was told what they
were up to he gave Onund and Yngvar an army and ordered
them to attack. There was heavy loss of life in the battle
before the chieftains fled. The one who had most opposed
paying the tribute was taken and hanged, but the others
got away. Onund and Yngvar won a great deal of booty for
themselves and after they had collected the tribute they came
back to King Olaf bringing him a vast fortune in gold, silver
and other treasures. This expedition made Yngvar so famous
that the king thought more highly of him than of any other
chieftain in Sweden.

Yngvar started keeping a concubine and had a son by her
called Svein. Yngvar remained in King Olaf's favour, but
when he was twenty, he grew melancholy and hardly spoke
a word. The king was very troubled by this and asked what
was wrong.

'If my melancholy really bothers you,' said Yngvar, 'and
if you really want to please me, then give me the title of king
and the honours that go with it.'

'I'll grant you anything else you want,' said the king,
'honours and riches, but that I can't do. I'm no wiser than
my forebears and I can't better them.'

This created tension between them, as Yngvar kept asking
for the title of king but got nowhere.

5. *Exploration*

Then Yngvar prepared for a journey overseas, for he wanted
to find a kingdom in some foreign land. He made his choice
of men and had thirty ships, all well fitted out. When King
Olaf heard that Yngvar was about to leave he sent messengers asking him to stay, and to take the title of king, but
Yngvar said he would only have accepted it, had the offer
been made sooner, and that he was now ready to sail once
he got a favourable wind.

A little later, Yngvar put out to sea with his thirty
ships and sailed from Sweden without lowering a sail
till he came to Russia. King Jarisleif gave him a great
welcome and Yngvar stayed there for three years, learning to speak a number of languages. He heard talk that
there were three rivers flowing through Russia from the
east, the one in between supposedly the largest. Yngvar
travelled widely in the east, asking everyone if they

could tell him where that river came from, but nobody knew.

From Russia, Yngvar prepared for an expedition to find the length of this river, and a bishop consecrated the steel and flint for him. Four of Yngvar's companions are mentioned by name: Hjalmvig, Soti, Ketil (an Icelander, nicknamed Ketil the Russian), and Valdimar. They launched their thirty ships into the river and Yngvar set course towards the east, with strict orders that no one was to go ashore without his permission, and that if anyone did so they would lose a hand or a foot. A man was ordered to keep watch by night on every ship.

The story goes that after they had been sailing for some time, it was Ketil's turn to keep watch one night. It seemed a long watch, with everyone else-asleep, so he thought he would go ashore and take a look round. He went further than he had intended, so he stopped short and looked about, and there right ahead of him he saw a tall house. He walked up to the house, went inside, and to his surprise he saw a silver cauldron over the fire, so he grabbed the cauldron and started running back to the ships. He had only gone a short distance when, glancing back over his shoulder he saw a fearsome giant chasing after him. He tried running faster but the giant kept gaining on him, so he threw down the kettle, though he kept hold of the handle, running as fast he could and glancing back from time to time. He saw the giant hesitate when he came to the kettle, reaching for it one moment and backing away the next. Eventually the giant picked up the kettle and went back to the house. When Ketil the Russian reached the ships, he broke the handle in two and put it into his sea-chest.

In the morning when the crew had woken up and gone ashore, they noticed the tracks leading from the ship, for there was dew on the grass, and told Yngvar about it. He asked Ketil if he had been ashore – for it could have been no one else – and promised not to kill him if he told the truth, so Ketil spoke up, said he was sorry for disobeying, and gave Yngvar the handle. Yngvar told him never to do it again, and they were friends once more.

So on they sailed for many days and through many regions until they began to notice that the animals' colours and habits were changing, evidence that they were getting further

away from their homelands, and one evening it seemed to
them that in the far distance they saw what appeared to
be a half-moon rising up from the ground. That night it
was Valdimar's turn to keep watch, and he went ashore to
investigate what they had seen. He came to a piece of rising
ground, golden in colour, and he saw that the cause of this
was a carpet of glittering dragons. All of them appeared to
be sleeping so he stretched out with his spear-shaft towards
a particular gold ring and pulled it towards him. At that, one
of the smaller dragons woke up and roused the others, till
the Jakulus himself was awake. Valdimar raced back to the
ships and told Yngvar what had happened, at which Yngvar
ordered his men to get themselves ready for the dragon and
move the ships into the harbour on the other side of the
river, and so they did. When they saw this terrible dragon
come flying across the river, most of them hid in terror.
The Jakulus flew above a ship captained by two priests, and
spewed so much venom on it that both ship and crew were
annihilated. After that it flew back across the river.

For some days Yngvar sailed up river, then a number of
towns and large settlements came into sight, and they saw
a fine city built in white marble. As they came closer they
were able to make out crowds of men and women. They were
much impressed with the beauty of the city, and the courtly
conduct of the ladies there, many of them very handsome.
But one woman was more beautiful and more elegantly
dressed than all the others, and this fine lady beckoned
Yngvar and his men to come and meet her. She asked
him who they were and where they were going, but Yngvar
made no reply as he wanted to know what other languages
she could speak. As it turned out, she spoke Romanic, German, Norse, Russian and many other languages current in
the east.

Once Yngvar knew that she spoke these languages, he
introduced himself and asked her own name and title.

'My name is Silkisif,' she said, 'and I am queen of this
land.'

She invited Yngvar and his men over to the city, an offer
he accepted, and the townsmen lifted their ships ashore,
rigging and all, and carried them up to the city walls. Yngvar
fitted out a great hall to stay in with all his men, but since
there was evidence everywhere of pagan customs, he locked

it securely, and forbade his men to mix with the heathen or allow any women into the hall apart from the queen. Some of his men paid little heed to his orders, but he had them put to death and after that no one dared to disobey him.

Yngvar spent a very enjoyable winter there, for every day the queen and her wise men would sit talking with him, exchanging all kinds of information. Yngvar would tell her about God's omnipotence, a faith very much to her liking, and she came to love Yngvar so deeply that she offered him her whole kingdom and with it the title of king, and finally offered to give herself to him so that he would settle down there. But he told her that, although he would accept her offer later on, he wanted first to explore the long river.

In the spring, Yngvar prepared to set out once more and took leave of the queen and her people. He sailed up-river until he came to a great waterfall in a narrow gorge with high cliffs, so that they had to haul the ships up by cables and after portage, refloat their ships. For some time they sailed without noticing anything in particular. Then late in the summer they saw a large number of boats coming towards them, round-shaped, with oars all around the gunwales and making straight for Yngvar's fleet: so, since they were going as fast as would a flying bird, he had no choice but to wait for them. As they approached, one of the men stood up, dressed in royal costume. He spoke in several languages but when Yngvar made no reply he said a few words in Russian. Yngvar understood that his name was Jolf, from a city called Heliopolis, and once King Jolf realised who Yngvar was, where he had come from and where he was intending to go, he invited Yngvar to stay with him throughout winter at his city. Yngvar declined the offer saying that he had no time to linger, but the king insisted he stay over the winter, so Yngvar had to agree.

They sailed their ships to a harbour where they disembarked, and travelled overland to the city. Looking back, they saw the townsmen carrying their ships on their backs right up to the city, where they could be kept under lock and key. In every street they saw many signs of heathenism, so Yngvar urged his men to pray earnestly and hold fast to their faith. Jolf gave them a hall and Yngvar kept such a close eye on his men that winter, not one of them defiled himself by having affairs with women or any other kind of heathen practice. They would take their weapons whenever they had to leave the hall, and kept it locked while they were away. No one from the city was allowed inside apart from King Jolf, but he used to sit there every day talking to Yngvar, each telling the other things old and new about their own countries.

Yngvar asked Jolf if he knew the source of the river, and Jolf said he knew for a fact that it flowed from a spring: 'We call it Lindibelti,' he said, 'and from the same spring another river flows into the Red Sea where it creates the huge whirlpool we call the Gapi. There's a tongue of land between the sea and the river, called Siggeum, and after the river has flowed only a short distance it pours down over the cliff into the Red Sea, and that's where we think the world ends. But this river you've been sailing along is the haunt of some unpleasant pirates with large ships which they cover with reeds so that people think they're islands. These men have all kinds of weapons and flaming missiles, and kill more people with fire than with weapons.'

The townspeople thought their king was neglecting his duties because of Yngvar, and threatened to depose him and choose another king. When Yngvar heard about this, he advised the king to do as his people wanted, and so he did. The king asked Yngvar to help him fight his brother, who was the more powerful of the two and had given Jolf a hard time. Yngvar promised that, when he came back from the east, he would help.

6. *The Giants*

When winter was over, Yngvar set sail with his men, all fit and well, away from Jolf's kingdom. After they had been sailing for some time they came to a massive waterfall, which created such a squall they had to make for land. When they reached the river bank, they saw the footprints of a huge giant, eight feet long. The cliffs were so high it was impossible to haul up the ships by their cables, so they pulled in closer to the cliffs where the current was not so strong, and they were able to scramble ashore through a narrow gap. The ground was flat and marshy, and Yngvar told his men to fell timber and make themselves digging tools, which is what they did. They started digging, making sure to keep the canal the right width and depth from the point they

were going to let the river flow into it. They worked at this
for months before they could take their ships through.

After they had been travelling for a long time they saw
a house, with a giant outside so fearsome and ugly they
thought it must be the Devil himself. In their great terror
they prayed to God for mercy and Yngvar told Hjalmvigi, a
most worthy cleric, to sing some hymns to the glory of God,
and they promised six days of fasting and prayer. Then the
giant walked away from the house, down towards the river,
and as soon as he was out of the way they went up to the
house. They could see that it had a stout wall round it, and
once they were inside they saw that it was supported by a
single pillar of clay. They set to work, hacking away at the
base of the pillar so that the whole house shook under the
assault. Yngvar told his men to look for large stones and
bring them up to the house, and that was what they did.
As dusk began to fall, Yngvar told them to hide behind the
wall and take cover among the reeds. Late in the evening
they saw the giant approaching, with a large number of
men dangling from his belt. He locked the gate in the wall
securely and did the same for the house, then settled down
to eat. After a while they tried to find out what he was up
to, and heard him snoring noisily, so Yngvar told them to
take the stones they had carried up and to hurl them at the
pillar until the building collapsed. The giant gave a violent
jerk and managed to free one leg, but Yngvar and his men
ran up and hacked it off, using axes, for it was as hard as a
tree. Once they saw the giant was dead, they hauled the leg
down to the ships and preserved it in white salt.

After that they travelled on until, where the river forked,
they saw five islands that stirred and then started moving
towards them. Yngvar told his men to prepare themselves,
then took some fire, lit from a consecrated tinder-box. Soon
one of the islands came up close to them and bombarded
them with a shower of stones, but they shielded themselves
and hit back. When the enemy realised how tough the oppo-
sition was going to be, they began blowing the bellows to fan
the flames of the furnace they had on board, which made a
great deal of noise. They also had a brass tube, from which
a great spark came flying: it landed on one of Yngvar's ships
and in no time at all burnt it to ashes. When Yngvar saw
this he grieved for his loss, then called for the tinder-box

with the consecrated flame. He bent his bow, strung an arrow and set to its tip the tinder-box with the consecrated flame. The arrow flew blazing from the string straight into the tube jutting from the furnace, and so the fire was turned against the heathen, and in the blinking of an eye the island was burned to ashes – men, ships and all. Then the other islands came up, but no sooner had Yngvar heard the sound of the bellows than he began shooting the consecrated flame, and with God's help destroyed these human devils, reducing them to cinders.

Not long after this, Yngvar reached the source of the river. There they saw a monstrous dragon, the like of which they had never seen, and under it a great hoard of gold. They approached land not far from the dragon and came ashore, walking till they reached the track it used when it crawled down to the water. They path was broad and Yngvar told his men to sprinkle salt all over it, then drag up the giant's leg for he thought that might make the dragon stay around for a while. After that they kept quiet and looked about for cover. Soon the time came for the dragon to crawl as usual to the water, and as it came along the track it saw the salt and began licking at it. When it got to the giant's leg it swallowed it down in one gulp. It was taking the dragon longer than usual to make the trip since three times, midway to its lair, it had to turn back to slake its thirst. Yngvar and his men made their way there, and saw a great quantity of gold as hot as if it had just been poured from a crucible. They used their axes to hack off a piece that alone was worth a fortune, then seeing the dragon coming up they hurried off with the gold and hid it among the reeds. Yngvar warned them not to be too curious about the dragon and most of them obeyed, but a few stood upright and saw the fury of the dragon over its loss, rising up on its tail, whistling like a human being and whirling round and round above its gold. These men described what they had seen, then dropped down dead.

7. Back to King Jolf

After that, Yngvar and his men set out once more and explored the headland on which they had come ashore. They discovered a fortified city where there was a great hall. In they went and found the hall richly furnished with many precious things. Yngvar asked whether anyone was willing to spend the night there and find out something about it, and Soti said he would be glad to do that. When it began to grow dark, Yngvar went back to the ships with his men while Soti found himself a place to hide.

Late at night, a demon in human form appeared to Soti, and this is what he said: 'Once upon a time there was a strong and forceful man called Siggeus, who had three daughters and endowed them richly with gold. He died and was buried just where you saw the dragon, but after his death the eldest sister so begrudged the others their gold and treasure, she killed herself, and the second sister did likewise. The third lived on and inherited her father's wealth, remaining in control of the estate even after her death. She gave the name of Siggeum to the headland. Every night she fills the great hall with demons, and I am one of them, sent to tell you this story. Dragons ate the bodies of the king and his daughters, and it was into dragons that some people believe they were transformed. Remember this, Soti, and tell your king, that King Harald of Sweden travelled this way long ago and was drowned in the Red Sea whirlpool along with all his followers: now he had come to take charge here, and to confirm my tale, I can tell you that his banner is kept here in the hall: Yngvar must take it and send it back to Sweden so that the people there will no longer be in the dark about what happened to their king. Tell Yngvar this, too, that he and most of his men will die on this expedition. You, Soti, an unrighteous, faithless man, must remain here with us, but Yngvar will be saved by his faith in God.'

After the demon had spoken he fell silent, though throughout the night there was plenty of racketing and roaring. Next morning Yngvar returned, and Soti told him what he had heard and seen, after which he dropped down dead before their very eyes.

At that, Yngvar took the banner that stood in the hall, went with all his men back to his fleet and turned his ships about. He gave a name to the great waterfall, calling it Belgsoti, and after that there is nothing to tell till they reached the land of King Hromund, or Jolf as he was also called. As they were sailing towards the city of Heliopolis, King Jolf came up towards them with a large fleet and asked Yngvar to lower his sails.

'Now you must give me your support to fight my brother,

57

Bjolf, also know as Solmund,' he said. 'He and his eight sons
want to rob me of my kingdom.'

Yngvar sailed on to the city and there his men prepared
for battle. He ordered the construction of some great wheels
with sharp nails and spikes sticking out all round, as well as
spiked iron balls. Now both sides gathered their forces and
met on an agreed field of battle, but by the time Yngvar had
formed up his troops it was clear that Bjolf had the greater
number of men. King Jolf drew up his men to face his
brother. When the two sides were ready they shouted the
war-cry, and Yngvar and his men released the wheels with
their deadly equipment against the enemy, and killed so
many that the line was broken. Then Yngvar attacked their
flank, killing all of the sons of Bjolf and putting Bjolf himself
to flight. King Jolf went off in pursuit and routed them, but
Yngvar told his men to stay put.

'We mustn't go so far from our ships that our enemies
might lay hands on them,' he said. 'Better to get plenty of
loot from the enemies we've killed here.'

They took a vast fortune in treasures of all sorts and
carried it down to the ships. Just then, Jolf came back
with his forces, formed them up and started shouting the
war-cry, which took Yngvar by surprise, forcing him to fall
back, but then he ordered his men to throw the spiked iron
balls in front of the feet of the enemy. They knew nothing
about this and ran forward, straight on to the spikes, thinking when they felt how sharp they were that it was all done
by witchcraft.

Yngvar made camp and picked up a fortune in treasure.
Then they saw a great crowd of women coming up towards
the camp, playing beautiful music, but Yngvar told his men
to keep away from these women as they would the most
venemous serpents. When it was growing dark and the men
were getting ready for bed, the women marched into the
camp, and the lady of the highest rank chose to sleep with
Yngvar, which so enraged him, he drew out a knife and
stabbed her in the private parts. When the other men saw
what he had done, some began chasing these loose women
away, but there were others who slept with them, unable to
resist their seductive charms and devilish witchcraft. When
Yngvar heard about this, all the pleasure he had taken in
wine and all his joy in silver turned into deep sorrow, for

when they called the roll next morning, eighteen of the men lay dead. After that, Yngvar gave orders for their burial.

8. *Death of Yngvar*

Then Yngvar and his men made hurried preparations to leave and were soon under way, travelling at speed by day and night as fast as they could. Then a sickness broke out, killing all his best men and more than half of his force. By the time Yngvar himself fell sick, they had reached Silkisif's kingdom. He summoned his men and told them to bury the dead, then called Ketil and other friends to his side.

'I've fallen sick, and expect it to be my death,' he said. 'I shall be going to the place that I have earned. I know that God is merciful and that His son will make good His promise, since I have placed myself daily in His hands, body and soul, and have done all that I could for my people. There's something I want you to know, that it is by the righteous judgement of God that I have been stricken with this disease. Both plague and witchcraft were directed more against me than the others, and when I am dead the plague will have run its course. I'm asking you men, particularly you, Ketil, to take my body back to Sweden and bury me there at church. Everything here that I possess, gold, silver and precious clothing, I want divided into three parts. One third I bequeathe to the church and the clergy, another to the poor, and the third part to my father and my son. To Queen Silkisif, bear my farewells. But more than anything else, I want you to agree amongst yourselves, and should there be any disagreement about which course to take, the decision must lie with Ketil since he has the sharpest mind.'

At that he bade them farewell, hoping to meet them again on the Day of Rejoicing, and spoke wisely about many things. After that he lived only a few more days.

His men prepared his body for burial and laid it in a coffin, then continued their journey, which ended at Citopolis. Recognising their ships, the Queen came to welcome them in great splendour, but as she watched them disembark she was troubled, and she feared that something terrible had happened for she could not see the man who was dearer to her heart than any other. She asked for news, exactly how Yngvar had died and what had happened to his body. When they said he had been buried, she called them liars and threatened to put them to death unless they told her the truth. At that, they told her what Yngvar had instructed them to do with his body and worldly possessions. They gave her Yngvar's body and she had it carried to the city in state, and embalmed in precious oil ready for burial, then told them they could go in God's peace, and in Yngvar's.

'Your God is my God too,' she said. 'When you get back to Sweden, bear my greetings to Yngvar's kinsmen. Ask for one of them to bring priests over here to convert my people to Christianity, then a church will be built here where Yngvar can be buried.'

Yngvar died in the year of Our Lord 1041 at the age of twenty-five: that was eleven years after the fall of King Olaf Haraldsson the Saint.

Ketil and the rest got ready to leave, and bidding farewell to the Queen, they set out with twelve ships. After they had been travelling for some time, there was disagreement as to which route they should take, and they split up, neither group being willing to follow the other. Ketil knew the right direction and got back to Russia, but Valdimar managed to reach Constantinople with a single ship: what happened to the rest we cannot say for sure, but people think most of them were lost. This is all we can tell you about Yngvar, though we know that he performed many great deeds on his expedition, as have been described by learned men.

This Ketil we have spoken of spent the winter in Russia, and travelled across to Sweden the following summer, where he gave an account of all that had happened on the expedition, handed over the property to Yngvar's son Svein, and brought him the greetings and message of the Queen. Svein was young in years, but very sturdy, strong and the image of his father. He wanted to test his own strength, setting out as a viking, and some years later he came with a large force east to Russia, where he spent the winter.

9. Svein's expedition

The story goes that Svein went to school that winter and learned to speak many of the languages known to be current in the east. Next, he fitted out thirty ships and said he meant to sail with this force to Queen Silkisif, taking with him a large number of priests under the leadership of a bishop called Rodgeir. The bishop blessed some dice three times, and three times he cast them, and each time the answer was that God wished him to go. The bishop said he would do so with pleasure.

Now Svein set out from Russia on his journey. After they had been travelling up-river for two days, the heathen suddenly appeared and attacked them with ninety ships of the type that the Norwegians call 'galleys'. Once the heathen had begun to fight, so did the others, but neither side could understand what the other was saying. While his men were putting on their armour, Svein appealed to God and threw the dice to find out His will, whether they should fight or flee from such overwhelming odds. The dice told him to fight, and Svein swore to give up the viking life if God would grant them victory. Then the fight began, and Svein and his men killed the heathen at will. The outcome was that the heathen fled in twenty ships, but the rest were killed, while Svein lost only a few men and won all the money he and his followers could have wished, in gold and all kinds of treasure.

They got under way again, travelling on until they came to where Ketil had got possession of the handle. Svein told his men to arm themselves and so they did. Soon after they saw a large farmstead with a huge man outside shouting in a loud, frightening voice. Then people, the so-called Cyclopes, began crowding in from every direction with great logs in their hands the size of house-beams. Though they had neither armour nor proper weapons they formed up for battle. Svein told his archers to start shooting right away and said there was no time to lose.

'For they're as strong as lions,' he said, 'and as tall as trees or houses.'

They shot away at the Cyclopes and killed a lot of them and wounded others, then something extraordinary happened, for the strongest of the Cyclopes began to run away. Svein ordered his men not to go after them, saying that there was no shelter, and they rushed instead to the nearest town and captured in the raid much of value in the form of furs, clothing, silver and all kinds of precious metals, after which they went back to their ships and carried on with the journey.

They had been sailing for some time when Svein noticed a creek cutting into the land, and told his men to steer towards

61

it. Since many of them were youngsters, they were only too keen to obey, and as they approached land they could see castles and a good many farmsteads. Then they caught sight of eight men running at astonishing speed towards them. One of the natives had a feather in his hand, and first he pointed up the stem of the feather, then the blade, which seemed to be a token of peace, so Svein responded with a hand-sign of peace too. The natives gathered under the lee-side of a cliff, offering various kinds of merchandise. Svein told his men they could go ashore, and they traded with the natives though neither side could understand what the other was saying.

Next day, Svein's men went ashore yet again to trade with the natives and for a while they exchanged goods, until one of the Russians tried to break an agreement he had just made to buy some furs. When the heathen lost his temper and punched him on the nose so that the blood poured onto the ground, the Russian drew his sword and sliced the heathen in two. At that the heathen people ran off shouting and screaming but in no time they gathered in what seemed an invincible army. But Svein told his men to arm themselves for war and march against the heathen, and in the fierce battle that followed the heathen, having no protective armour, fell in huge numbers. When they saw that they had lost the battle, the heathen ran, and Svein and his men won a great deal of plunder left behind by the others, which they carried down to the ships.

Praising God for their victory, Svein and his men set out once more, travelling for some time. Then they saw a large herd of pigs at the foot of a bluff on a headland jutting out into the river. Some of the men raced ashore to hunt the pigs. They caught some, but the pigs started squealing noisily and bolted inland. Next thing, they saw a great host coming towards the ships, led by a man walking well ahead of the rest and carrying three apples. Suddenly he threw one of them into the air and it landed right at Svein's feet: then he threw another and it hit the same spot. Svein wasn't going to wait for the third apple.

'There's some diabolical power and weird custom behind all this,' he said.

He put an arrow to his bowstring and shot: the arrow struck the man on the nose with a sound like the shattering

of horn, and the heathen threw back his head, and they could
see then that he had a beak like a bird. He began screaming
loudly and ran back to his people, and they all raced inland as
fast as they could, and that was the last Svein saw of them.

10. More trouble with the Heathen

After that Svein turned back to his ships and yet again they
got under way, but they had only sailed a short distance that
day when they saw ten men leading some kind of beast, a
very strange creature it seemed to them, for on its back was
a tall wooden tower. Those of Svein's men who were most
curious to find out what manner of beast it was went ashore,
fifty of them in all. When the natives leading the creature
saw them coming, they abandoned it and ran off to hide.
Sveins' men went up to the animal and tried to lead it away,
but it lowered it's head and refused to budge from the spot,
though they all tugged at the reins that hung from its head.
They thought there must be some secret device they knew
nothing about, since ten natives had been able to lead it, and
decided to leave the creature alone and hide among the reeds
where they could keep an eye on it. A little later the natives
reappeared. They went up to the creature, took hold of the
reins and laid them on either side of the neck, then through
a hole in a certain cross-beam on the tower. They were able
to raise the beast's head by means of the pulley in the hole.
Once Svein's men saw the animal was on its feet again they
rushed up to it as fast as they could, took charge of it, and
led it wherever they wanted. However, since they had no
idea what kind of creature it was or what food it required,
they speared it to death then went back to their ships and
rowed off.

The next thing they saw was a great crowd of heathen on
the river bank making peace signs, so at once Svein made
for the shore and found a good harbour. Between them they
organised a market where Svein bought many things of great
value. Then the heathen invited their customers to a feast in
a certain house, and they accepted. Entering, they saw all
kinds of delicacies and the very best of drink. Svein's men
sat down at table and blessed themselves, but when the heathen saw the sign of the cross they went crazy and attacked
them, some using their fists, others going for their hair. Both
sides were calling for help, and when Svein heard his men

shouting and saw them brawling he said, 'Who knows? This meeting may turn out very badly for us.'

Then he went to his men and told them to get their weapons and armour. When they had formed up, they saw that the heathen had done the same, but bore a bloodstained man before them as their banner. Svein consulted Bishop Rodgeir and asked him what should be done.

'If the heathen expect the corpse of some evil man to bring them victory,' said the bishop, 'let us consider it our duty to trust in the aid of Heaven, where Christ Our Lord dwells in His Mercy, the leader of the faithful and guardian of us all, both living and dead. Bear before you the victory sign of Our Christ the Crucified and call upon his name – that will bring us victory, and death to the heathen.'

When the bishop had spoken these rousing words, they took the crucifix and image of Our Lord, and bore it as a banner before the army. They marched against the heathen without fear, while the priests went aside to pray, and when the two armies met, the heathen were struck blind and many were in terror, scattering in every direction – some into the river, others into fens and forests, perishing in their thousands.

After the enemy had been routed, Svein had the dead buried, and afterwards warned his men not to show any curiosity about heathen practices.

'On this expedition,' he said, 'we've lost more in men than we've gained in profit.'

11. Death of a Dragon

Once more Svein set out, and they travelled on until they came to the place where the half-moon had seemed to stand upon the earth. There they made for land and went ashore. Ketil told Svein what had taken place when he was there with Yngvar. Svein ordered his men to hurry from the ships and confront the dragon. They set off and came to a great thicket near to the dragon's lair, where they hid. Svein sent out several youngsters to spy out what they could of the dragon, and they saw lots of little dragons lying asleep, with the Jaculus encircling them all. One of the men stretched out the shaft of a spear to pick up some gold ring, and the shaft touched one of the little dragons, which woke up and roused the one

64

nearest, and so each roused another until the Jaculus itself reared up.

Svein was leaning against a great oak-tree, and set onto his bow-string an arrow with tinder the size of a man's head on the tip, made with consecrated fire. When he saw that the Jaculus was in the air flying towards the ships with its jaws gaping, he shot the arrow with the sacred fire straight into its mouth and right into its heart. The dragon crashed dead to the ground, at which Svein and his men rejoiced, praising God.

12. The Queen

Svein told his men that they needed to get away fast because of the foul stench of the dead dragon, so they raced back to their ships, all but six who had been curious enough to examine the dragon and had dropped dead on the spot. Though these were the only ones killed by the dragon's stench, most of the others were in agony because of it. So Svein hurried to get away from there, and carried on with his journey until he reached the land of Queen Silkisif, where she came out to meet them in grand style. After they had disembarked, Ketil was the first to greet the queen but she paid no attention to him and turned towards Svein, trying to kiss him. He pushed her away and said he had no desire to kiss her, a heathen woman.

'Anyway,' he asked, 'why should you want to kiss me?'

'Yours are the only eyes here like Yngvar's that I can see,' she replied.

The travellers were given a fine welcome, and when she learned that they had a bishop with them Silkisif was very pleased, though he had to preach the faith to her through an interpreter since he did not understand her language. Soon she had attained enough spiritual understanding to receive baptism, and within a month all her people had been baptized.

Shortly after, the Queen held a large meeting to confer with her people, and it was here that Svein Yngvarsson was robed in purple, and a crown set upon his head. The people all accepted him as their king, and he married the queen.

13. A new church

After the wedding feast, King Svein and his queen travelled
in state through their kingdom, with the bishop and priests
among their retinue, for along with this land, King Svein
converted to Christianity all the others that had been under
the queen's dominion. When summer came, and aided by
the divine power of mercy the entire country had embraced
the faith, King Svein and his men wished to prepare for their
journey back to Sweden so that they could tell their kinsmen
about the expedition. The queen realised this, but asked
Svein to send his men back to Sweden and remain behind
himself.

'I'm not going to send my men away without me,' Svein
answered, 'there are great dangers of many kinds to be
faced by those who go on this journey. The same thing may
happen as before when there was no leader, and the whole
army perished or lost its way.'

The queen listened to his words, and could see that he
had made up his mind.

'If I have my way,' she said, 'you won't leave just yet. It
may be that you'll never return to this country, or perhaps
be killed by one of those perils you spoke of. Think of your
duty, too, to sustain the faith and build more churches. First
of all you must build in the city a great minster, and if it's
as grand as I should like it to be, there your father's remains
shall be buried. After that, three years from now, you may
go in peace.

The queen had her way. Svein stayed on for three years
and before the time was up a great church had been completed in the city. Then the queen sent for the bishop, and
when he was enrobed, he asked:

'In whose name, queen, do you wish this church to be
dedicated?'

'This church,' she said, 'shall be dedicated to the glory of
the holy King Yngvar, who rests here.'

'But why?' asked the bishop. 'Has Yngvar shone in
miracles since his death? The only men we can call saints
are those who shine in miracles after their bodies have been
buried in the earth.'

'I've heard it from you yourself,' she replied, 'that the
steadfastness of true faith and the constancy of holy love are

66

worth more in the eyes of God than the glory of miracles. And I know from my own experience that Yngvar was steadfast in the holy love of God.'

When the queen had said that this should be, the bishop dedicated the minster to the glory of God and all His saints, including Yngvar. Then a stone coffin was hollowed out and Yngvar's remains laid in it, with a precious cross, finely wrought, standing over the coffin. The bishop had frequent masses sung for the soul of Yngvar, and gave the people leave to call it Yngvar's Church.

14. Authorities and informants

When all this had been done, Svein prepared to leave, and travelled all the way north to Sweden where the people gave him a friendly and honourable welcome and invited him to rule the kingdom. He listened to their offer but would have none of it, saying that he had won for himself a better and richer kingdom to which he soon meant to return: and two years later, Svein sailed away from Sweden.

Ketil stayed behind. He said he had heard that Svein spent the following winter in Russia, prepared to continue his journey in the spring. At the height of summer, Svein started out from Russia and nothing has been heard of him since he set sail up river.

Ketil went back to Iceland, settling there amongst his kinsfolk, and he was the first to tell of these events. But we have heard that some saga-men claim that Yngvar was the son of Eymund Olafsson, thinking it to have been a greater honour for him to have been a king's son. Onund would gladly have given his whole kingdom to buy back Yngvar's life, for all the chieftains in Sweden wanted Yngvar as their king. Now, some people may ask what it is that shows Yngvar was not the son of Eymund Olafsson, and this is how we would wish to reply: Eymund, son of Olaf, had a son called Onund, and this Onund was very like Yngvar in character as well as in his travels far and wide, as is stated in a book called *Gesta Saxonum*:

'It is said that Eymund, King of the Swedes, sent his son Onund across the Baltic Sea to the most vicious Amazones, and that he was killed by them.'

Some people say that Yngvar travelled for two weeks, seeing no light apart from the candles they had with them because the overhanging cliffs closed over them above the river, and that for these two weeks it was as if they were rowing through a cave. However, learned people think this very unlikely, unless the river was flowing through a narrow gorge where the cliffs narrowed above the water, or the trees were growing so densely above the cliffs that they overlapped. But though that is possible, it is not very likely.

We have heard this story told, but in writing it down we have followed a book composed by the learned monk Odd, which he based on the authority of well-informed people mentioned by him in his letter to Jon Loftsson and Gizur Hallson. Those who believe they know better must augment the account wherever they think it wanting. The monk Odd says he heard this story told by a priest called Isleif, and also by someone called Glum Thorgeirsson, and he had a third informant named Thorir. Odd took from each of these whatever he thought most interesting. Isleif told him that he had heared this story from a certain trader who claimed to have heard it at the royal court of Sweden. Glum had the story from his father, Thorir from Klakka Samsson, while Klakka learnt it from his older kinsmen.

And so we end this saga.

EYMUND'S SAGA

1. Eymund Hringsson

There was a king called Hring who reigned in the Uplands in Norway, and the kingdom he ruled over was called Hringariki. A wise man, popular, generous and very wealthy, he was the son of Dag, son of Hring, son of Harald Fine-hair. Descent from him was held to be the best and noblest in Norway.

Hring had three sons, who all became kings: the eldest called Hraerek, the next Eymund and the third Dag. They were all valiant men and had charge of their father's defences; they added to their fame by going on viking expeditions as well.

Our story is set around the time King Sigurd Sow reigned in the Uplands. He was married to Asta Gubrand's-daughter, mother of King Olaf Haraldsson the Saint. She had a sister, Thorny, who was the mother of St Hallvard, and her other sister, Isrid, was maternal grandmother of Thorir of Steig. When Olaf Haraldsson and Eymund Hringsson reached manhood they became blood-brothers. They were much the same age, trained in every sport that makes for a better man, and they would stay alternately with King Sigurd and King Hring, Eymund's father.

When Olaf set off for England, Eymund went with him, and they were joined by many other men of distinction, including Ragnar son of Agnar, who was the son of Ragnar Rykkil, son of Harald Fine-hair. The more widely they travelled, the greater grew their reputations, as demonstrated by King Olaf the Saint whose name is a by-word throughout the northern world. When Olaf came to the throne of Norway, he conquered the whole country and did away with all the provincial kings, as told in his saga along with other events recorded by learned men. According to Styrmir the Learned, the story is that he dethroned eleven kings in Norway, five of them in a single morning. Some of them he had put to death, some crippled, some banished from the land. Hring, Hraerek and Dag were caught in this upheaval, but Eymund and Earl Ragnar Agnarsson were on a viking expedition when it was all taking place.

Hring and Dag left the country and were engaged in war for many years, after which they went east to Gautland and ruled there for a long time. King Hraerek, however, was blinded and held at King Olaf's court until he betrayed the king, setting his retainers man against man by means of slander so that they began killing one another: on Ascension Day, Hraerek made an attempt on King Olaf's life in the choir of Christ's Church, cutting the fine cloak he wore, but God came to the king's aid and he was unhurt. But King Olaf was so angry about this that he ordered Thorarin Nefjulfsson to take Hraerek to Greenland, if winds were favourable. But they put in at Iceland and Hraerek went to stay with Godmund the Wealthy at Modruvellir in Eyfjord, and later he died at Kalfskinn.

2. Eymund and Ragnar

Now, next to tell is that shortly after this Eymund and Ragnar arrived in Norway with a large fleet. King Olaf was nowhere near at the time. They were given the news of what had happened, as we have just described it, and Eymund called a meeting of his fellow-countrymen, whom he addressed in this manner:

'Since we left, things of the gravest significance have taken place in the land. Our kinsmen have been lost to us, some of them driven from the land under torture. The loss of our noble and distinguished kinsmen is both an injury to us, and an humiliation. Once there were many who ruled in Norway, now there is only one, but while my blood-brother Olaf is in charge I think the realm is in good hands, even though his rule is considered to be something of a tyranny. I expect him to treat me with all honour, except for the title of king.'

Mutual friends suggested that Eymund should meet with King Olaf and see whether he would grant him the title of king.

'I'll not bear arms against King Olaf,' replied Eymund, 'to join the ranks of his adversaries, but in view of the matters standing between us, I've no intention of making any plea for

mercy or laying down my claim to a royal title. So since I don't
mean to make a peace-settlement with him, what else can I do
but keep my distance? I know that if we were to meet he would
grant me high honours, for I'll never attack his kingdom, but
I'm not sure matters would stand so well with you, men, your
kinsmen having been so much dishonoured: and if you were to
invite me to act, it would place me under a great strain since I
would have been made to swear oaths of allegiance, and would
be duty-bound to keep them.'

'If you don't want to come to terms,' said Eymund's men,
'apart from staying well away from the king, and leaving your
possessions for a life in exile, and not joining the ranks of his
enemies, what do you have in mind?'

'Eymund has spoken much to my own way of thinking,'
said Ragnar. 'I wouldn't trust our fortune against King Olaf's
luck. But I think we should see to it, if we're to abandon our
own estates, that people think we've made a better bargain
than others have.'

'If you're willing to follow the scheme I have in mind,' said
Eymund, 'I'll tell you what, with your agreement, I think we
should do. I've heard that east in Russia King Valdimar has
died, and his kingdom is in the hands of his three sons, all
good men. King Valdimar divided the kingdom between them
unevenly, one son having a larger share than the other two. The
one who inherited most is the eldest, Burislaf – the second is
called Jarisleif and the third Vartilaf. Burislaf has Kiev, the
best realm in all Russia, while Jarisleif has Novgorod, and
Vartilaf Polotsk and all the region around. But they haven't
yet come to an agreement about their territories, and the one
who is least happy with his lot is the one who got the biggest and
best share. Because his kingdom is smaller than his father's,
which he considers a loss, he thinks himself a lesser man than
his forebears. Now, what I have in mind is that, as long as you
agree, we go to Russia, visit these kings, and stay with one of
them, preferably one who intends to hold on to his realm but
is satisfied with the way their father divided the country, for
we're sure to win fame and fortune there. Now I'd like us to
make a firm decision on the matter.'

And that was what they all wanted. Many of them were
keen to make money, and had suffered ill-treatment in Norway. They would rather leave the country than stay behind
and put up with harsh conditions laid on them by the king

and their enemies, so they chose now to join Eymund and Ragnar, who sailed east to the Baltic with a large force of hard, handpicked men.

King Olaf heard nothing of this till they had gone, and said it was a great pity he and Eymund had not met.

'For we would have been even better friends at parting,' he said, 'but it's only to be expected that he should feel hostile towards us: now the man is gone to whom we would have granted every honour but the title of king.'

King Olaf had been told what Eymund had said at the meeting, and said Eymund was just the man to make the right decision: and since there is no more to tell of this, we now return to the story of Eymund and Ragnar.

3. Eymund arrives in Russia

Without breaking their journey, Eymund and his men travelled to Novgorod in the east to King Jarisleif, whom they visited first at the request of Ragnar. King Jarisleif was son-in-law to King Olaf of Sweden, being married to his daughter Ingigerd. As soon as the king heard of their arrival he sent messengers bearing an offer of safe conduct and an invitation to a lavish feast, which they accepted gladly.

At the feast, the king and queen questioned Eymund closely about King Olaf Haraldson of Norway, to which he replied that there was much to be said in praise of him and his way of life, and that they had long been blood-brothers and close companions. But he said nothing about the things he disliked, which we have already mentioned.

Eymund and Ragnar formed a high opinion of the king, and no less of the queen, for she was a woman of great presence and generous with money too. As to money, King Jarisleif was not considered especially open-handed, though he was a good ruler and a man of spirit.

4. Eymund and Jarisleif discuss terms

Now King Jarisleif asked them about the plans they had for their journey, and how far they meant to travel.

'Sir,' they replied, 'we've heard that because of your brothers, you may be forced to reduce the size of your kingdom. We, in turn, have been driven out of our own land, which is why we came here to Russia in the east to see you and your brothers. We have a mind to offer our allegiance to the one who grants us the highest honour and rank, since it's fame and fortune we're seeking, and we look to receive honour and distinction from you. It struck us that you'd wish to have brave men about you, should your honour come under attack from those kinsmen of yours, the very men who are turning into your enemies. Now, we're offering to take charge of the defences of the kingdom and become your hired soldiers, taking payment from you in gold, silver and fine clothes. Should you decide to give us a quick refusal and turn down our offer, we'll accept the same terms from another king.'

'We're badly in need of your support and counsel,' replied King Jarisleif, 'you Norwegians are brave and intelligent men. But it's still not clear to me how much pay you're asking in return for your services.'

'First of all,' said Eymund, 'you're to provide us and all our troops with a great hall, and see to it that we'll never be without the very best of your provisions if we should want them.'

'That's what I want,' said the king.

'These men,' said Eymund, 'will be at your disposal, to go ahead of your own troops in battle, in defence of the kingdom. You'll also pay every one of our soldiers an ounce in weight of silver, and to each Captain an additional half-ounce.'

'We can't have that,' replied the king.

'Yes you can, sir,' said Eymund. 'We'll take payment in kind, beaver pelts and sable furs and other things readily available in your kingdom. We, not our men, will set a value on it. And as long as there's plenty in the way of spoils you should be able to pay us out of that, but if we sit around doing nothing there'll be less pay.'

So the king agreed to this, and that was how matters stood for the next twelve months.

5. *War in Russia*

Now Eymund and his men beached their ships and made them fully secure. King Jarisleif had a stone-built hall prepared for them, hung with the costliest tapestries, and they were provided in the most generous fashion with all they might need. Each day they spent with the king and queen, having a fine time and enjoying themselves, but they had not been entertained there very long before King Jarisleif received letters from King Burislaf demanding certain district and market towns nearby on the grounds that they were conveniently situated for raising

73

revenue. King Jarisleif told King Eymund what his brother had asked for.

'There's little that I can suggest,' replied Eymund, 'but you're welcome to our support if you want it. If your brother means well, you'll need to go along with his wishes, but if, as I suspect, he's going to ask for more once this has been granted, then you're faced with a choice whether or not to surrender your kingdom. Will you hold on to it like a real chieftain and fight your own brother to the bitter end, with the resolve to hold on to your position afterwards? It's less hazardous to give him what he wants, but there are many who would think it cowardly and unbecoming a king if you were to do that. I don't see the point, either, of maintaining foreign troops here if you don't put your trust in us. Now, the choice is yours.'

King Jarisleif said he wasn't inclined to surrender his kingdom without making an effort.

Then Eymund said, 'That's what you must say to your brother's messengers, that you're going to defend your kingdom, but don't give him time to build up his army against you. Wise men have said that there's more luck in fighting on one's own soil that on someone else's.'

The envoys went back and reported to their king all that had taken place, that King Jarisleif was not going to share any part of his kingdom with his brother, and was ready for battle should King Burislaf decide to attack.

'He must be expecting reinforcements if he means to fight it out with us,' said the king. 'Were there perhaps some foreigners with him giving him advice and strengthening his kingdom?'

The messengers said that they had heard some Norwegian king had arrived with six hundred fellow-countrymen.

'They must have been the ones who gave the king this advice,' said King Burislaf, and now he started gathering his own forces.

King Jarisleif despatched the war-arrow to all parts of his kingdom, so now both kings were mustering their troops, and things turned out just as Eymund had expected. King Burislaf led his troops across the border against his brother and they faced one another in a great forest, by a broad river on either side of which they made camp. Neither army outnumbered the other. King Eymund and the Norwegians pitched their tents away from the rest, and for four days all remained quiet, neither side attacking the other.

Then Ragnar asked, 'What are we waiting for, what's the point of sitting around?'

'Perhaps our king is underestimating the enemy,' replied Eymund. 'His plans aren't very good.'

After that, they went to see King Jarisleif and asked him whether he had any intention of doing battle.

'It seems to me we've a fine army,' said the king, 'we've strong troops and trusty.'

'That, sir, is not the way I see it,' said Eymund. 'When we first got here it seemed to me there were only a few men to each tent on the other side and that the camp had been planned to take many more troops than were actually there. But now things have changed: they've had to enlarge their camp and pitch tents outside it, while many of your troops have run off home and the army can't be relied on.'

'What can we do?' asked the king.

'Things are much less easy now than they were,' said Eymund. 'Sitting here, we've let victory slip through our fingers. Still, we Norwegians have managed to do something. We've moved all our ships up-river along with our armour. We're going to make our way across the river with our troops and lead them to the rear of the enemy camp, leaving our tents empty. You and your men must begin hitting the enemy right away.'

And that's what happened. The trumpets were blown for the attack, the banners were raised, and each side formed up for battle. Now the armies clashed, and savage fighting began with heavy loss of life. Eymund and Ragnar made a fierce onslaught on King Burislaf and his men, taking them from the rear. It was the hardest of battles with severe casualties, but then King Burislaf's army began to break ranks and his men took to their heels. King Eymund strode forward amongst his troops, killing so many of the enemy that it would take long to list them by name. Now the enemy was routed, offering no resistance, those who escaped with their lives running into the woods and fields, and at the same time it was reported that King Burislaf had fallen. After the battle, King Jarisleif took massive spoils.

Most people attribute the victory to King Eymund and the Norwegians. They earned from it a mighty reputation, to be expected in the circumstances, for God the Lord Jesus Christ judged rightly, as He does in all things. After that they went back home and King Jarisleif enjoyed both his kingdom and all the spoils of battle.

6. *Eymund gives advice*

The rest of the summer and the winter which followed were quiet, and nothing happened, King Jarisleif ruling over both kingdoms with the help of King Eymund. The Norwegians were now held in high honour and respect as the king's defensive shield, advising him and winning him plunder. However, they received no pay from the king, who thought himself less in need of support now that the other king was dead and his whole kingdom seemed at peace.

When the time for payment ran out, Eymund went to see King Jarisleif and this is what he said.

'Sir, we have stayed here in your kingdom for a while: now you must decide whether our agreement is to continue, or whether you would prefer us to part company, and my men and I seek another chieftain. The pay has been slow in coming.'

'I don't think I need your support as much as before,' said the king. 'It would ruin us to give you as much pay as you're asking for.'

'That's true, sir,' said King Eymund. 'since now you'll have to pay each of my men an ounce of gold, and a half-mark of gold to every captain.'

'In that case,' said the king, 'our contract's over.'

'That's up to you,' said King Eymund. 'But are you quite sure that Burislaf's dead?'

'I think so,' said the king.

'He must have a magnificent tomb,' said Eymund, 'so where was he buried?'

'We don't exactly know,' replied the king.

'It would become your nobility, sir,' said Eymund, 'to know where such an honoured man as your brother lies buried. But I suspect your men have given you a one-sided report without being fully informed on the matter.'

'What do you know about this that comes nearer the truth, and that we ought to trust more?' asked the king.

'I've been told King Burislaf is alive,' said Eymund, 'staying over the winter in Permia, and we've heard from a trustworthy

76

source that he's gathering a large army to lead against you.
That's nearer the truth.'

'When will he reach our kingdom?' asked the king.

'I've heard that he'll be here in three weeks,' replied
Eymund.

And now King Jarisleif had no wish to lose their support,
so the contract was extended for twelve months.

'What's to be done now?' the king asked next. 'Should we
gather troops and go into battle?'

'Yes, that would be my advice,' replied Eymund, 'if you
want to defend Russia against King Burislaf.'

'Should we keep the troops here or lead them out against
the enemy?' asked the king.

'We must summon them all here to the town,' replied
Eymund, 'and once the army's assembled, we'll devise some
likely scheme which will suit our purposes.'

7. *The battle between the brothers*

Next, King Jarisleif sent a war summons to every part of the
kingdom, and a large army of farmers gathered. After that,
King Eymund sent his men into the woods to fell trees, bring
them to the town, and set them up on the ramparts of the
fortress, with the branches of all the trees facing outwards
so that people could not shoot missiles into the fort. He
also had a great ditch dug all round the fort and filled with
water after the earth had been carried away. Next he placed
branches over it and covered it in such a way that the earth
appeared undisturbed. When this had been completed, they
learned that King Burislaf had reached Russia and was on
his way to the town where King Jarisleif and King Eymund
were waiting.

King Eymund and his men had made two of the town gates
particularly secure, where they intended to make their stand
and, if need be, their escape. During the evening before enemy
troops were expected, King Eymund told the women to go
up onto the ramparts of the fort with all their jewels and after
settling themselves comfortably there, to hang all their heavy
gold bracelets on poles and so create an impression.

'I'm sure the Permians will be eager to lay hands on the
jewellery,' he said, 'and when the sun shines on the gold and
the precious gold-woven cloth, they'll be wild to charge the
stronghold.'

Things were arranged as he had asked. Burislaf led his troops out of the forest towards the town, and they saw how splendid it was. And now, assuming there had been no news of their coming, they rode headlong towards it hard and warrior-like. A great many of them fell into the moat and died there, but King Burislaf was in the rear, and realised there had been a disaster.

'Maybe this place isn't to be won as easily as we expected, and these Norwegians have a few tricks up their sleeves,' he said.

Now that all the splendour on display had vanished, he considered what would be the best place to attack. He saw that all the town gates were shut except for two, and they were not going to be easy to get through, being well prepared against attack and heavily defended. The war-cry rang out, but the townspeople were ready for battle, with each of the kings, Jarisleif and Eymund, ready at his gate.

A fierce battle followed, with heavy losses on both sides, and the pressure was so intense on the gate defended by King Jarisleif that the enemy managed to force a way through. The king received a bad leg-wound and there were many casualties, before the gate was taken by the enemy.

'Things are looking bad,' said King Eymund. 'Our king has been wounded, a lot of our men have been killed, and now they're breaking through into the town. Ragnar,' he said, 'decide what you're going to do, defend the gate here or go and help our king.'

'I'll stay here,' answered Ragnar. 'You join the king, your advice is needed over there.'

Eymund went with a large body of men and saw that the Permians had now made their way into the town, so he attacked them fiercely and killed a number of King Burislaf's troops, pushing forward hard and keenly, urging on his men: and considering the time it lasted, never was there such a ferocious onslaught. Now all the Permians still on their feet ran from the town, and King Burislaf took to his heels too, his troops suffering heavy casualties. King Eymund and his men drove them into the forest, killing the king's standard-bearer, and yet again King Burislaf was reported killed, so this was a famous victory. In this battle, King Eymund greatly enhanced his reputation, but now things quietened down. The Norwegians stayed on with King Jarisleif in great honour, and everyone there thought very highly of them, but still the soldiers' pay was slow to arrive and hard to come by, and on the appointed day it was still overdue.

8. More trouble over pay

One day, it so happened that King Eymund had a word with King Jarisleif, saying that he should pay their wages in a manner befitting a great ruler. He added that he thought they had put more money into his hands than all the pay they were due.

'We think you're making a big mistake,' said Eymund, 'and won't be needing our support and service any longer.'

'It may be that things will go well for us now,' said the king, 'even without your support. You may have been a great help to us, but from what I hear, your forces are altogether inadequate.'

'Why should it be, sir, that only you should be the judge of everything?' asked Eymund. 'There are plenty of my men who think they've suffered very badly, some losing a leg or an arm or some other part of the body, others their weapons. All this costs a great deal of money. You can still pay compensation, and must make up your mind one way or the other.'

'I don't want you to leave,' said the king, 'but we're not paying you as much when there's no likelihood of war.'

'We need money,' replied Eymund, 'and my men want more than food for their service. We'd rather go to another country and seek our fortune there – it's not likely there'll be war in your kingdom, though are you quite sure King Burislaf is dead?'

'We have his banner,' said the king, 'so we think it's true.'

'What do you know about his burial?' asked Eymund.

'Nothing,' replied the king.

'It's not very clever to know nothing,' said Eymund.

'Do you know any more about it than other people,' asked the king. 'Those who know the facts?'

'It was easier for him to lose his banner than his life,' said Eymund, 'and I understand that he escaped and has been in Turkey over the winter. Now he means to lead yet another army against you. He's gathered an unbeatable army with Turks, Wallachians and a good many other nasty people, and I've also heard that he's quite likely to give up his Christian faith and hand over both kingdoms to these unpleasant people should he manage to take Russia away from you. If he has his way, he'll drive all your kinsmen out of the country for sure, and humiliate them.'

'How soon will he be here with that ugly lot of his?' asked the king.

'In a couple of weeks,' replied Eymund.

'Now what are we going to do?' asked the king. 'We can't manage without your foresight.'

Ragnar said that he wanted to leave, and told King Jarisleif to consider for himself what was best.

'If we were to abandon the king in such a dangerous situation,' said Eymund, 'we'd be asking for criticism. The king was at peace when we first came to him. I won't leave him now unless he can live in peace after we're gone. Better extend our contract with him for another twelve months, but as we stipulated at the time, he must increase our pay. Now we must work out our plans: should we muster an army? Or would you prefer us Norwegians alone to defend the country, sir, and not involve yourself in our battles, and only use your troops should we be defeated?'

'That's the way I want it,' said the king.

'Don't be so hasty, sir,' said Eymund, 'there's another way of handling the matter. It would be more proper to keep our armies together, I think, and we Norwegians won't be the first to run, though I know there are plenty who will, once they're facing the spear-points. What I don't know is how the people who are keenest to get into action will behave when it comes to the real test. What's to be done, sir, if we come face to face with the king, shall we kill him or not? There'll be no end to this war while you're both alive.'

'I won't be two-faced,' said the king. 'I'll not urge my men to fight King Burislaf and then complain if he's killed.'

So now they returned home each to his own hall, without either of them mustering troops or making preparations of any kind, which everyone thought very peculiar, to make no preparations when things were most threatening. A little later they heard that King Burislaf had arrived in Russia with a great army, including a number of rough elements. King Eymund made out that he knew nothing of what was going on, as if he'd not heard about it, and there were plenty of people who said that he lacked the courage to fight Burislaf.

9. *Eymund kills Burislaf*

Early one morning, Eymund summoned his kinsman Ragnar and ten other men to join him. He had horses saddled for them, and they rode off from the town, only twelve of them, leaving the rest behind. One of his companions was an Icelander called Bjorn, another was Ketil of Gardar, and there were two men called Thord, and one called Askel.

Eymund and his men had an extra horse with them to carry their arms and provisions and off they rode, all of them dressed as merchants. Nobody knew the purpose of the journey or what it was they were up to. They rode as far as a certain forest, then carried on all day until nightfall. When they were out of the forest they came to a great oak, and beyond it, a fair, broad, level clearing.

'We'll break our journey here,' said King Eymund. 'I've heard King Burislaf plans to camp here and spend the night.'

They passed beyond the oak up to the clearing and looked for the best place to pitch their tents.

'This is where Burislaf is going to camp,' said King Eymund. 'I've heard that he always sets up his tents near a wood, if he can, so that he can use it as an escape route should he need to.'

King Eymund took a length of rope or cable and told his men to go into the clearing – 'right up to this tree,' he said – then asked one of them to climb up into the branches and tie the rope there, which was done. Next they bent the tree until the branches were right down to the ground, and so the whole tree right down to the root.

'I like it,' said King Eymund, 'and it may proved handy for us.'

Then they took the rope ends and secured them, and it was mid-evening by the time all this had been completed. Just then they heard King Burislaf's men arriving, and retired into the forest where their horses were. They could see a large number of men and a fine chariot, well accompanied, with a banner carried ahead. These people made for the forest, straight into the clearing and up to the best camping spot, just as King Eymund had calculated, where they pitched their main tent, sitting the rest of the camp some way off at the edge of the forest. All this occupied them till it was dark. The royal tent was beautifully made and richly decorated, with four wings and towering above it a tall pole with a golden ball and a wind-vane.

From the forest, Eymund and his men watched all that was being done by the army and stayed silent. When it was dark, fires were lit in the camp and they knew that food was being prepared there.

'We're short of provisions,' said Eymund, 'which is rather inconvenient, so I'll go to their camp and see what I can manage in the way of catering.'

Eymund dressed himself up as a beggar, fixed a goat's beard to his face, and off he went on two sticks. He walked into the royal tent and began begging for food from everyone there. After that, he went to the nearest tents and was given ample hospitality for which he offered his thanks, and then made off from the camp well stocked with provisions. After the troops had eaten and drunk all they wished, all was quiet.

King Eymund divided his men into two groups, six in the first group to see to the horses and make sure they were ready should they be needed in a hurry: but he himself and five companions strolled into the camp as if they hadn't a care.

'Rognvald, Bjorn and the Icelanders,' said Eymund, 'you're to go to the place where we tied down the tree.'

He gave each of them a wood-axe. 'You know how to strike a good blow,' he said. 'Now's the time to do it.'

They went to the spot where the branches had been bent over.

'The third man is to stand here on the path to the clearing,' he said. 'All he needs to do is to hold the rope, and loose it to us when we pull it towards us, for we'll be holding the other end. And when everything is just the way we want it, the man I've given the job to must give the rope a tap with the handle of the axe. The man who's holding the rope must be clear whether it quivers because of the blow, or just because we've given it a tug. Now, if luck is on our side, once this sign has been given, which must be made at the crucial moment, the man holding the other end of the rope must acknowledge it. Then the branches of the tree are to be cut, and the tree will shoot up powerfully into the air.'

They did all that they had been told, then Eymund and Ragnar, accompanied by Bjorn, went up to the royal tent and made a slip-knot on the rope. With the aid of spear-shafts, they managed to loop it over the vane at the top of the pole above the tent, sliding it up as far as the knob. They went about this very quietly, while all the troops in the camp were fast asleep, exhausted by the journey and very drunk.

When all this had been done, Eymund and his men short-ened the rope by pulling at the ends. Then Eymund went up close to the royal tent as he wanted to be near when the tent was snatched up. There was a tap on the rope and as the one who held the other end felt it quiver, he warned those whose job it was to strike the blow: next, they cut the tree loose, and it shot up high, pulling the royal tent forcibly from the ground and hurling it far into the forest. At that, all the lights went out.

King Eymund had worked out during the night exactly where King Burislaf was sleeping in the tent, and hurried across to him, dealing him and a number of his followers their death blows. Then Eymund and his men ran off into the forest where they could not be found, taking with them King Burislaf's head. After all that had happened, King Burislaf's men were in a state of panic.

Eymund and his men rode back home without breaking their journey, arriving early in the morning, and going straight to King Jarisleif with the true facts of King Burislaf's death.

'Here, sir,' he said, 'is Burislaf's head, if you can recog-nise it.'

When he saw it, the king flushed red.

'We Norwegians are the ones who've performed this mighty task, sir,' said Eymund, 'and now you must prepare your brother's remains fittingly for burial.'

'What you've done comes as a shock,' said King Jarisleif, 'and touches me very closely. You must make the arrange-ments for his burial, but what action do you think his followers will take now?'

'It's my guess that they'll hold a meeting,' answered Eymund, 'and every one of them will suspect the others, as they knew nothing at all about us. None of them is going to believe anyone else, so they'll break up in confusion and form groups amongst themselves, and I don't think many of them will bother about burying their king.'

After that, the Norwegians set out from the town, riding the same path as before through the forest, until they reached the camp. Everything turned out exactly as Eymund had pre-dicted. King Burislaf's troops had all dispersed, having split up in disagreement. Eymund went into the clearing where the king's body lay, but there was no one else anywhere near it, so they made it ready for burial, place the head upon the trunk, and brought it to the town. Many people learned about his burial and the whole population of the country swore their allegiance to King Jarisleif, who now reigned over the two kingdoms that he and his brother had previously held.

10. Eymund parts from Jarisleif

The summer passed and the following winter, but nothing happened about the pay that was due. The king was told by a number of people that there had been a great deal of talk about the killing of his brother, and the Norwegians now thought the king lived in fear of them.

On the day it had been agreed that the Norwegians would receive their pay, they went to the royal chambers, where the king welcomed them and asked what they wanted so early in the morning.

'Maybe you're no longer in need of our service, sir,' said Eymund, 'so now it's time to hand over the pay that's due to us.'

'Your coming has had serious consequences,' said the king.

'That's true, sir,' replied Eymund. 'You'd have been driven out of your kingdom long ago without our help, and as for the death of your brother, the situation hasn't altered for you yourself approved it.'

'What are you going to do now?' asked the king.

'What's the last think you'd want us to do?' enquired Eymund.

'I don't know,' replied the king.

'I know exactly,' said Eymund. 'The last thing you'd want is for us to go to your brother King Vartilaf: so now we'll go to him and give him all the support we can, sir, and good luck to you.'

At that they marched rapidly down to their ships, which were all ready to sail.

'That was a sudden departure,' said the king, 'and not what I wanted.'

'What's going to happen if you and King Eymund are on opposite sides?' asked the queen. 'He'll be a hard man to deal with.'

'It would be good to get rid of them,' said the king.

'Before that happens, they're going to humiliate you,' replied the queen.

Then she went with Rognvald Ulfsson and several others down to Eymund's ships, which were lying just offshore. Eymund learned that the queen wanted a word with him.

'We can't trust her, she's cleverer than the king,' he said, 'but I'll not refuse to speak to her.'

'In that case I'll join you,' said Ragnar.

'No,' said Eymund, 'this isn't a hostile visit, there's no need for a whole army.'

Eymund was wearing a cloak with straps and had a sword in his hand. They sat on a raised bank down on some mudflats, the queen and Earl Rognvald so close to him they were almost sitting on his clothes.

'It's sad that you and the king are parting in this way,' said the queen. 'I'd gladly do all I can to see that you get on better with one another.'

Neither of them had kept their hands idle: Eymund had untied the straps of his cloak and the queen had pulled off one of her gloves and was waving it above her head. Eymund realised this wasn't entirely innocent, and in reality she had arranged for some men to kill him, her glove being raised as a sign to them. At once these men made for him, but before they could reach him he had seen them and jumped to his feet faster than they expected, leaving his cloak behind. They had lost their chance.

Ragnar saw what was going on and raced ashore from the ship followed by one after another of the Norwegians, all intent on killing the queen's men, but Eymund would have none of it. They pushed the men off the mudbank and laid hands on them.

'We're not arguing with you about what we should do,' said Ragnar to Eymund, 'we're taking the queen and her men off with us.'

'If we did that we'd be wrong,' replied Eymund. 'Let them go home in peace, I'll not ruin my friendship with the queen.'

So now the queen went home, not very pleased with her excursion, while the Norwegians sailed off without delay to the kingdom of Vartilaf. When they went to see him he gave them a friendly welcome and asked the news. Eymund told him all that had happened from start to finish, when he had parted company with King Jarisleif.

'What do you plan to do next?' asked the king.

'I told King Jarisleif we were coming here to see you,' replied Eymund. 'I've a feeling that he'll want to reduce the size of your kingdom just as his brother did to him. It's up to you, sir, to decide whether you want us here, and whether you think you need our support.'

'Yes indeed, we'd very much like your support,' said the king, 'but what would you want in return?'

'We want the same terms that we had from your brother,' replied Eymund.

'Give me time to talk it over with my men,' said the king. 'They're the ones who will have to lay out the money, even though I hand it over.'

King Eymund agreed, and King Vartilaf summoned his men to a meeting. He told them the news he had been given, that his brother Jarisleif was planning to attack his kingdom, and that King Eymund had turned up with an offer of his support and protection. They urged the king to take in the Norwegians, and a bargain was struck. The king adopted Eymund as his own special counsellor.

'I'm not as clever a fellow as my brother Jarisleif,' he said, 'and you got the better of him. We'd like to have regular discussions with you, and we'll pay you strictly according to the agreement.'

So the Norwegians stayed there in high regard, hospitably entertained by the king.

11. The brothers make peace

It so happened that envoys came from King Jarisleif, demanding from King Vartilaf certain towns and villages that lay close to his kingdom. King Vartilaf consulted Eymund about the matter.'

'It's your decision, sir,' answered Eymund.

'Now I must remind you,' replied the king, 'it was agreed that you would advise me.'

'As I see it,' said Eymund, 'you must expect a hard fight from a killer-wolf, sir, and once the lesser thing has been granted, the greater will be demanded. But send the envoys back in peace. The king and queen will think they know what we have in mind. How long do you need to muster your forces?'

'A fortnight,' replied the king.

'Now, sir,' said Eymund, 'you must say where you want to face your brother in battle, and let the envoys know so that they can tell their king.'

So that was done, and the envoys returned home. Both sides prepared for battle and met at the pre-arranged spot near the border, where they set up camp, but did nothing more for several days.

'Why are we sitting here doing nothing?' asked King Vartilaf. 'Victory's within our reach.'

'Let me have my way in this,' replied Eymund. 'It's always best to put off a bad thing, and Queen Ingigerd hasn't appeared yet. Even though the king is commander of the army, she's the one who's really in charge. Now, sir, I'll keep watch.'

'As you wish,' said the king.

For seven days they waited there with the army. One night when the weather was foul and it was very dark, King Eymund and Ragnar slipped away from their troops and disappeared into the forest behind King Jarisleif's camp, where they sat down by the side of a certain path.

'This path must be used by King Jarisleif's men,' said Eymund, 'and if I had wanted to travel secretly this is the one I'd use. Let's wait here for a while.'

Just after they'd been sitting there for some time, and Eymund had said, 'It's not very clever sitting here,' they heard people, one of them a woman, riding past. They saw there was a man riding ahead of a lady, with another man behind.

'This must be the queen,' said Eymund. 'Let's position ourselves on either side of the path, and when they reach us, you wound the horse she's riding, Ragnar, and get hold of her.'

As the riders went past, they had no idea what was happening until the queen's horse fell dead and she vanished completely, though one of them said he had caught a glimpse of a man slipping across the path. They dared not face the king and had no idea whether men or trolls were responsible for what had happened, so they went off without having seen anyone.

'You Norwegians,' said the queen to the blood-brothers, 'you don't easily give up the idea of humiliating me.'

'We'll treat you well, queen,' replied Eymund, 'but I don't think you'll be kissing the king for a while yet.'

87

They went to King Vartilaf's camp and told him that the queen had arrived. He was delighted, and watched over her himself. Next morning she sent for King Eymund and when they met she spoke first.

'It's best,' she said, 'that we come to a settlement, and I am prepared to act as arbitrator, though first I must declare that I wholly favour King Jarisleif.'

'This is a matter for King Vartilaf to decide,' said Eymund.

'But your words carry most weight with him,' she replied.

So then Eymund went to see King Vartilaf and asked whether he agreed that the queen should arbitrate.

'I don't think it would be wise,' said the king, 'since she's declared herself to be against our interest.'

'Would you be content to keep what you have?' asked Eymund.

'Yes,' replied the king.

'I wouldn't call it arbitration if you don't keep the larger share,' said Eymund. 'You've as much right as Jarisleif to inherit from your brother.'

'You're in favour of accepting her arbitration then,' said the king. 'So let it be.'

Eymund told the queen that it had been agreed she should settle terms between the kings.

'It must have been your advice,' she said. 'Now you'll see what's to be done and who has the fewer shortcomings.'

'I didn't object to your being granted the honour,' said Eymund.

Then the trumpet was sounded for a meeting, and it was announced that the Queen Ingigerd would speak with the kings and their men, but when the armies gathered people could see that Queen Ingigerd was in the company of King Eymund and the Norwegians.

It was proposed on behalf of King Vartilaf that the queen should act as arbitrator, and she told King Jarisleif that he should have the best part of Russia, that is, Novgorod.

'But Vartilaf shall have Kiev,' she said, 'the second best kingdom, with all its dues and taxes, twice as much as Vartilaf had before. As for Polotsk and the lands belonging to it, they shall be given to King Eymund to rule over and he shall receive all the revenues intact, for we don't wish him to leave Russia. Should there be heirs on the death of Eymund, they must inherit the kingdom, but were he to die without issue, the kingdom must revert to the brothers Jarisleif and Vartilaf. King Eymund shall be in charge of the defences of the land on behalf of both brothers and of all Russia, and in return they must support him with all the power at their command. King Jarisleif is to be overlord of Russia as a whole, and Earl Rognvald to rule over Ladoga Town as he has done in the past.'

This settlement, and the territorial divisions, were confirmed and approved by everyone there, with Queen Ingigerd and King Eymund to arbitrate on all issues. After that, they all returned to their kingdoms.

King Vartilaf ruled for only three years, a very popular king, but then he fell sick and died. King Jarisleif took over after his death and ruled alone over both kingdoms. King Eymund ruled over his own kingdom, but he lived to no great age and died peacefully, leaving no heirs. His death was considered a great loss by the people, for there has never been a wiser foreigner in Russia than King Eymund, and there was no war in Russia as long as he was in charge of King Jarisleif's defences. As he lay sick, King Eymund handed over his kingdom to his blood-brother Ragnar, wanting him rather than any other to have the benefit of it. This was done with the approval of King Jarisleif and Queen Ingigerd.

Rognvald Ulfsson, first cousin to Queen Ingigerd, was earl of Ladoga, a great chieftain and tributary to King Jarisleif, and lived to a ripe old age. When King Olaf Haraldsson the Saint was in Russia, he stayed with Rognvald Ulfsson and there was a deep friendship between them, for King Olaf was held in high respect by all men of honour while he was in Russia, though by no one more than Earl Rognvald and Queen Ingigerd, between whom there was a secret love affair.

LIST OF PROPER NAMES

The following abbreviations are used: *YS* (Yngvar's Saga): *ES* (Eymund's Saga). The numbers refer to chapters, not pages.

Agnar Ragnarsson, *ES* 1
Aki, a Swedish Chieftain, *YS* 1–2
Amazones, *YS* 14
Askel, *ES*, 9
Asta Gudbrand's-daughter, *ES* 1
Aud, daughter of Earl Hakon of Norway, *YS* 1

Baltic, *YS* 14; *ES* 2
Belgsoti, a waterfall in the East, *YS* 7
Bjolf, brother of Jolf, *YS* 7
Bjorn, an Icelander in Russia, *ES* 9
Burislaf, a king in Russia, brother of Jarisleif, *YS* 3; *ES* 2, 5–9

Christ, *YS* 10; *ES* 5
Citopolis [var. Scitopolis], *YS* 8
Constantinople [Mikligarðr], *YS* 8
Cyclopes, *YS* 9

Dag Hringsson, Eymund's brother, *ES* 1
Dag Hringsson, Eymund's grandfather, *ES* 1

Eirik the Conqueror, King of Sweden [*c*.950–993], *YS* 1–2
England, *ES* 11
Eyjafjord, Iceland, *ES* 1
Eymund, son of Aki, *YS* 1–3
Eymund Hringsson, *ES passim*
Eymund Olafsson, *YS* 14

Gapi, a whirlpool, *YS* 5

List of Proper Names

Gesta Saxonum, *YS* 14

Glum Thorgeirsson, one of Odd Snorrason's informants, *YS* 14

Gizur Hallsson, an Icelandic scholar [d.1197], *YS* 14

Gotaland, now part of Sweden, *YS* 1; *ES* 1

Greenland, *ES* 1

Gudmund the Powerful, an Icelandic chieftain, *ES* 1

Hakon, Earl of Norway [*c*.970–995] *YS* 1–2

Hallvard, a Norwegian saint, *ES* 1

Harald Fine-Hair, King of Norway [d.933], *ES* 1

Harald, King of Sweden (?), *YS* 7

Heliopolis, a city in the East, *YS* 5, 7

Hjalmvig, a priest, one of Yngvar's companions *YS* 5–6

Hrærek Hringsson, brother of Eymund, *ES* 1

Hring Dagsson, ruler of Hringariki, *ES* 1

Hring Haraldsson, *ES* 1

Hringariki, a province in Norway, *ES* 1

Hromund, an alias for King Jolf, *YS* 7

Iceland, *YS* 14; *ES* 1

Icelanders, *ES* 9

Ingigerd, daughter of King Olaf the Swede, *YS* 2–3; *ES* 3, 10–11

Isleif, one of Odd Snorrason's informants, *YS* 14

Isrid Gudbrand's-daughter, *ES* 1

Jaculus, a flying dragon, *YS* 5, 11

Jarisleif, King of Russia, *YS* 3, 5; *ES* 2–11

Jolf, a king in Russia, *YS* 5–6

Jon Loftsson, an Icelandic chieftain and scholar [d.1197], *YS* 14

Kalfskinn, a farm in Iceland, *ES* 1

Ketil of Gardar [Garda-Ketill], Yngvar's Icelandic companion, *YS* 5, 8–9, 14; *ES* 9

Kiev [Kænugarðr], *ES* 2, 11

Klakka Samsson, Thorir's informant, *YS* 14

Ladoga Town [Aldeigjuborg], *ES* 11

Lindibelti, the source of a major river in the East, *YS* 11

Modruvellir, a farm in Iceland, *ES* 1

Norway, *YS* 1–2; *ES* 1–2

Norwegians, *ES* 4–5, 7–11
Novgorod [Holmgarðr], *YS* 3; *ES* 2–3, 11

Odd Snorrason, an Icelandic author, *YS* 14
Olaf Haraldsson the Saint, King of Norway [1015–30], *YS* 8; *ES* 1–3, 11
Olaf, King of Sweden [999–1022], *YS* 1–5
Olaf Tryggvason, King of Norway [995–1000], *YS* 3
Onund, son of Eymund, *YS* 14
Onund Olafsson, King of Sweden [1022–1050], *YS* 3–4, 14

Permia [Bjarmaland], *ES* 6
Permians [Bjarmar], *ES* 7
Polotsk [Palteskja], *ES* 2, 11

Ragnar Agnarsson, Eymund's blood-brother, *ES*, 1–3, 5, 7, 9–10
Ragnar Rykkil Haraldsson, *ES* 1
Red Sea, *YS* 5, 7
Rodgeir, a bishop, one of Svein's companions, *YS* 9–10
Rognvald Ulfsson, a Norwegian earl, *ES* 10–11
Russia [Garðariki], *YS* 1, 3, 5, 8–9, 14; *ES* 2, 4, 7–8, 11

Scandinavia [Norðrlönd], *YS* 3
Semgalls [Seimgalir], *YS* 3
Siggeum, a headland in the East, *YS* 5
Siggeus, a fictitious king, *YS* 7
Sigrid the Haughty, wife of King Eirik of Sweden, *YS* 1
Sigurd Sow, ruler of the Uplands, *ES* 1
Silkisif, a Russian queen, *YS* 5, 8–9, 12
Solmund, an alias for Bjolf, *YS* 7
Soti, one of Yngvar's companions, *YS* 5, 7
Styrbjorn, a Swede, *YS* 3
Styrmir the Learned, an Icelandic scholar [d.1245], *ES* 1
Svein Yngvarsson, *YS* 4, 8–14
Sweden, *YS* 1, 3–5, 8, 14; *ES* 3

Thorarin Nefjulfsson, an Icelander, *ES* 1
Thord, two of Eymund's companions bear this name, *ES* 9
Thorir, one of Odd Snorrason's informants, *YS* 14
Thorir of Steig, a Norwegian chieftain, *ES* 1
Thorny Gudbrand's-daughter, *ES* 1
Turkey [Tyrkland], *ES* 8
Turks, *ES* 8

A GLOSSARY OF SAGAS
AND OTHER ICELANDIC TEXTS

Abbreviations used:
HP Hermann Palsson
IF Islenzk Fornrit
MM Magnus Magnusson
PE Paul Edwards

Ævi Snorra goda ('Life of Snorri the Priest', d. 1031). Presumably by Ari the Learned. Edited in *IF IV* (Reykjavik 1935).

Alexanders saga. A prose rendering into Icelandic of Galterus de Castellione's *Alexandreis*, a noble epic about Alexander the Great. The Icelandic translator, Brandur Jónsson, was Abbot of the Augustinian house at Thykkvabær in Ver 1247–62, and Bishop of Hólar 1263–4. *A.s.* was edited by Finnur Jónsson (Copenhagen 1925).

Alfrædi Islenzk. A modern title for a collection of medieval Icelandic treatises on geography, history, theology, natural history, mathematics, computistics, etc. Based on various authorities. Edited in three volumes by K. Kaalund (Copenhagen 1908–18).

Annales Regii or *Konungsannáll.* A late thirteenth-century compilation, but probably based on an earlier annal, now lost. Edited by Gustav Storm in *Islandske Annaler indtil 1576* (Christiania 1888).

Arrow-Odd. See Örvar-Odds saga, Fornaldarsögur Norðurlanda; translation in *Seven Viking Romances.*

Bandadrápa. A poem of praise by Eyjólfur dádaskáld, composed at the end of the tenth century.

Bjorn's Saga: Bjarnar saga Hitdælakappa. An early thirteenth-century story of a young Icelander who goes abroad, visiting Scandinavia, Russia, England and other foreign parts. During Bjorn's absence from Iceland the unscrupulous Thord marries his fiancée and a good many years later becomes his killer. Edited by Sigurdur Nordal in *IF III* (Reykjavik 1938).

A Glossary of Sagas and other Icelandic Texts

Book of Settlements. See *Landnámabók.*

Bosi and Herraud: Bósa saga og Herrauds. An entertaining fictitious tale about heroic adventure, magic and love. See *Fornaldarsögur, Seven Viking Romances.*

Breta sögur. A thirteenth-century Icelandic translation of Geoffrey of Monmouth's *Historia Regum Britanniae.* The translator's identity is unknown, but the narrative includes Gunnlaugur Leifsson's *Merlinusspá* (q.v.). See also *Hauksbók.*

Edda: The Prose Edda: Snorra-Edda. A handbook for poets, providing a wealth of information about myth, heroic legend, poetic diction and verse forms. It was written by Snorri Sturluson (d. 1241), probably about 1225. Several editions, including Finnur Jónsson, *Edda Snorra Sturlusonar* (Copenhagen 1931). Translated by Anthony Faulkes, *Snorri Sturluson. Edda* (London 1987).

Egil and Amund: Egils saga einhenda og Asmundar berserkjabana ('The Saga of Egil One-Hand and Asmund the Berserks-Killer'). A fictitious adventure story about two blood-brothers who set out on a perilous journey in search of a pair of abducted princesses. See *Fornaldarsögur, Seven Viking Romances.*

Egils saga Skallagrímssonar. Edited in *IF II* (Reykjavik 1933); translated by HP and PE as *Egil's Saga* (Penguin 1976).

Eirik's Saga: Eiriks saga rauda ('The Saga of Eirik the Red'). Written *c.* 1260, this tale describes the settlement of Greenland late in the tenth century and subsequent explorations of Vinland. Edited by Olafur Halldórsson in *IF IV (Vidbætir)* (Reykjavik 1985). See *The Vinland Sagas.*

Eiriks saga hins viðförla ('The Saga of Eirik the Far-Travelled'). A fourteenth-century tale about a young Norwegian who sets out in search of the Odáinsakur, a kind of Earthly Paradise. Some of the material that went into its making was borrowed from learned foreign books. Edited by Helle Jensen (Copenhagen 1984).

Eymundar saga: Eymund's Saga. Also known as *Þáttur af Eymundi og Ólafi konungi.* See the Introduction.

Eyrbyggja saga. Edited by Einar Ol. Sveinsson in *IF IV* (Reykjavik 1935); translated by HP and PE as *Eyrbyggja Saga* (Penguin 1989).

Færeyinga saga. An early thirteenth century work dealing with the history of the ruling families in the Faroes during the period around 950–1050. Edited by Olafur Halldórsson (Reykjavik 1967 and 1988). Translated by George Johnston as *The Faroe Islanders' Saga* (Toronto 1975).

First Grammatical Treatise. An anonymous treatise on the pronunciation and spelling of Icelandic *c.* 1150. Edited and translated by Hreinn Benediktsson (Reykjavik 1972).

Flateyjarbók. A modern title for a magnificent vellum codex written *c.* 1382–7 by two known scribes for a wealthy farmer in the north

A Glossary of Sagas and other Icelandic Texts

of Iceland. It contains several poems, including *Noregs konunga tal* and *Hyndluljód*, but its fame rests chiefly on its many sagas, among them *Eiriks saga vidförla*, *Ólafs saga Tryggvasonar*, *Ólafs saga helga*, *Orkneyinga saga*, *Færeyinga saga*, *Jómsvikinga saga*, *Sverris saga*, *Hákonar saga Hákonarsonar*, *Eymundar saga*, and many others. Edited in three volumes by C.R. Unger and Gudbrand Vigfússon (Christiania 1860–68), and by Sigurður Nordal (Akranes 1944–5).

Flos peregrinationis. A travel book by Gizur Hallsson (d. 1206), no longer extant.

Fornaldarsögur Norðurlanda ('Tales from the Remote Scandinavian Past'). The modern and somewhat misleading blanket title for a group of fictitious stories set in Scandinavia and beyond, but never in Iceland itself. Some, e.g. *Völsunga saga* are based on ancient heroic poetry, others have a less respectable background. Their historical value is slight, and it is hard to draw a line between them and the *riddararsögur* or 'tales of knighthood'. There is a popular edition in four volumes by Gudni Jónsson (Reykjavik 1950).

Gisla saga Súrssonar. Edited by Björn K. Þórólfsson in *IF VI* (Reykjavik 1943); and by A. Loth in *Membrana Regia Deperdita* (Copenhagen 1960). Translated by George Johnston as *The Saga of Gisli* (London 1963).

Göngu-Hrólfs saga. A fictitious tale of adventure and suspense, probably written about the beginning of the fourteenth-century. See *Fornaldarsögur*. Translated by HP and PE as *Göngu-Hrolf's Saga* (Edinburgh 1980).

Grettis saga Ásmundarsonar. Edited in *IF VII (Reykjavik 1936)*; translated by Denton Fox and HP as *Grettir's Saga* (Toronto 1974).

Hákonar saga Hákonarsonar. A biography of King Hákon of Norway (d. 1263). Edited and translated by Gudbrand Vigfússon and G.W. Dasent in *Icelandic Sagas* (Rolls Series 88, 2 and 4). See *Flateyjarbók*.

Halfdan Eysteinsson: Hálfdanar saga Eysteinssonar. Another fictitious tale for entertainment. See *Fornaldarsögur*, *Seven Viking Romances*.

Hauksbók. An important vellum codex, written *c.*1306–08, partly by its first owner, Haukur Erlendsson (d. 1334). It covers a wide range of subjects, including historical works such as *Landnámabók*, *Kristni saga* and *Eiriks saga rauða*, and translations from Latin: *Trójumanna saga*, *Breta sögur*, *Merlinusspá*, and *Elucidarium*. It also contains some interesting material of foreign origin on theology, history, geography, natural history, mathematics and computistics. Edited by Finnur Jónsson and Eirikur Jónsson (Copenhagen 1892–6). See *Alfrædi Islenzk*.

Heimskringia ('The Orb of the World'). A modern title: originally, the book was probably called *Sögur Noregs konunga*, 'The History of the Kings of Norway'. Written by Snorri Sturluson (d. 1241) around

A Glossary of Sagas and other Icelandic Texts

1235, it deals with the lives of rulers of Norway from legendary times to 1177. After a brief Prologue, the narrative begins with *Ynglinga saga*, where Odin himself and then his descendants are at the centre of things. Edited in three volumes by Bjarni Adalbjarnarson in *IF XXVI–XXVIII* (Reykjavik 1941–51). Translated by Samuel Laing in two volumes: *The Olafs sagas* (London 1964) and *Sagas of the Norse Kings* (London 1961).

Heiðarviga saga. Edited by Sigurður Nordal in *IF III*; (Reykjavik 1938) translated by William Morris and Erikur Magnusson as *The Heath-Slaying Story* (Saga Library II, London 1892).

Helga þattur þórissonar. See *Fornaldarsögur, Seven Viking Romances*.

Hord's Saga: Hardar saga og Hólmverja. A fictive story about an Icelandic outlaw of the tenth century. In its present form the saga can hardly be older than the beginning of the fourteenth century, but it appears to have been based on a thirteenth-century version no longer extant, which was more factual than the one we have. Translated by Alan Boucher as *The Saga of Hord and the Holm-Dwellers* (Reykjavik 1983).

Hrafnkels saga Freysgoda. Edited by Jón Jóhannesson in *IF XI* (Reykjavik 1950); and by Jón Helgason (Copenhagen 1950); translated by HP in *Hrafnkel's Saga and Other Stories* (Penguin 1971).

Hungurvaka ('An Appetizer'). The lives of the first five bishops of Skálholt (1056–1176). Edited by Jón Helgason in *Byskupa sögur 1* (Copenhagen 1938). Translated by Gudbrand Vigfusson and F. York Powell in *Origines Islandicae I* (Oxford 1905).

Hversu Noregur byggðist ('How Norway was won'). A mythical account of the beginning of Norwegian society. In *Flateyjarbók*.

Hyndluljóð ('The Lay of Hyndla'). An early narrative poem, including some fantastic elements. Its principal interest lies in the genealogical information it contains. Edited by Finnur Jónsson in his *De gamle Eddadigte* (Copenhagen 1932), and elsewhere.

Islendingabók ('The Book of the Icelanders'). Edited by Jakob Benediktsson *IF I* (Reykjavik 1969); translated by Halldór Hermannsson in *Islandica XX* (Ithaca, N.Y. 1930).

Islendingasögur ('Sagas of the Icelanders'). Commonly considered to be the greatest of the sagas; the characters they present are not only native Icelanders, but on the whole belong to lower social classes than the heroes of the *fornaldarsögur, konungasögur*, and *riddarasögur*, and some of them are written in a naturalistic mode reminiscent of the novel.

Islenzk fornrit (IF). A major series of edited texts intended to include most of the literature of medieval Iceland. So far twenty volumes have appeared.

Jómsvikinga saga. A story of action and violence, about a band of Vikings based in the Baltic, near the estuary of the River Oder. It

A Glossary of Sagas and other Icelandic Texts

is set late in the tenth century and was probably written early in the thirteenth. Edited by Olafur Halldórsson (Reykjavik 1969). Shorter version was edited and translated by N.F. Blake as *The Saga of the Jomsvikings* (Edinburgh 1962).

Jóns saga biskups. This deals with the life and miracles of the first bishop of Hólar (1106–21). Edited and translated by Gudbrand Vigfusson and F. York Powell in *Origines Islandicae I* (Oxford 1905).

Knytlinga saga ('The History of the Kings of Denmark'). Covers the period from the tenth century to the beginning of the thirteenth, probably written about the middle of the thirteenth. Edited by Bjarni Gudnason in *Danakonunga sögur, IF XXXV* (Reykjavik 1982). Translated by HP and PE as *Knytlinga Saga. The History of the Kings of Denmark* (Odense 1985).

Konungsannáll. See *Annales Regii.*

Konunga sögur ('Sagas of Kings'). Under this blanket term belong historical narratives relating to the kings of Norway and Denmark and to the earls of Orkney. See *Hákonar saga Hákonarsonar, Heimskringla, Knytlinga saga, Orkneyinga saga, Olafs saga helga, Olafs saga Tryggvasonar, Sverris saga,* etc.

Kormáks saga. Edited in *IF VIII* (Reykjavik 1939); translated by W.G. Collingwood and Jón Stefánsson as *The Life and Death of Cormac the Scald* (Ulverston 1902).

Kristni saga ('The History of Christianity'). Describes missionary activity in pagan Iceland, the Conversion in the year 1000, and the evolution of the national Church down to the early twelfth century. Edited and translated by Gudbrand Vigfusson and F. York Powell in *Origines Islandicae I* (Oxford 1905).

Laxdæla saga. Edited in *IF V* (Reykjavik 1934); translated by MM and HP as *Laxdæla Saga.* (Penguin 1969).

Landnámabók ('The Book of Settlements'). Describes the colonisation of Iceland *c.*870–*c.*930. There are three medieval versions, one of them fragmentary. The earliest version still extant was compiled by Sturla Pórdarson (1214–84). Edited by Jakob Benediktsson in *IF I* (Reykjavik 1969); translated by HP and PE as *The Book of Settlements* (Winnipeg 1972).

Leidarvisir ('Sign-post'). A guide for Icelandic pilgrims going to Rome or the Holy Land. It was written by Abbot Nikulás Bergsson of Munkaþverá, who travelled to both places *c.*1150. Edited in *Alfrædi Islenzk I* (q.v.).

Life of Snorri the Priest. See Ævi Snorri goda.

Lifssaga Olafs hins helga. See Olafs saga hins helga.

Magnúss saga Eyjajarls. Edited in *Orkneyinga saga* (q.v.); translated by HP and PE as *Magnus' Saga: the life of St Magnus Earl of Orkney 1075–1116* (Perpetua Press, Oxford 1987).

Merlinusspá. See Breta sögur.

A Glossary of Sagas and other Icelandic Texts

Njáls saga. Edited in IF XII (Reykjavik 1954); translated by MM and HP as *Njáls Saga* (Penguin 1960).

Noregs konunga tal ('Succession of the Kings of Norway'). A late twelfth century poem about Norwegian rulers from the tenth century to the time of its composition. Edited by Finnur Jónsson in *Den norsk-islandske Skjaldedigtning I* (Copenhagen 1912).

Olafs saga hins helga ('The Saga of King Olaf the Saint'). Several sagas were written about King Olaf Haraldsson of Norway (d. 1030), the earliest in the late twelfth century. Of particular interest are Styrmir Kárason's *Lifssaga Olafs hins helga* (*c.*1220–30), of which numerous fragments survive, and Snorri Sturluson's *Olafs saga hins helga* (*c.*1230), which also exists in abridged form in *Heimskringia*. Greatly extended versions of the saga are to be found in *Flateyjarbók* and elsewhere.

Olafs saga Tryggvasonar. The earliest version of the *Saga of Olaf Tryggvason* are two translations of Odd Snorrason's *Vita Olavi*, written *c.*1190. Both were edited by Finnur Jónsson: *Saga Olafs konungs Tryggvasonar af Oddr Snorrason munk* (Copenhagen 1932). Much better known is Snorri Sturluson's *Olafs saga* in his *Heimskringia*. A greatly extended version of the saga is to be found in *Flateyjarbók* and elsewhere. See Olafur Halldórsson's edition, *Olafs saga Tryggvasonar hin mesta I-II* (Copenhagen 1958–61).

Orkneyinga saga ('The History of the Earls of Orkney'). Deals with the rulers of Orkney from the ninth century to the end of the twelfth. Edited by Finnbogi Gudmundson in *IF XXXIV* (Reykjavik 1965); translated by HP and PE as *Orkneyinga Saga* (Penguin 1981).

Orvar-Odds saga ('The Saga of Arrow-Odd'). A fictitious tale about a great adventurer who travels far and wide and lives to be three hundred years' old. See *Fornaldarsögur, Seven Viking Romances*.

Páls saga biskups. A biography of Bishop Páll Jónsson of Skálholt (1195–1211). Edited by Jón Helgason in *Byskupa sögur 2* (Copenhagen 1978); translated by Vigfusson and Powell, see *Hungurvaka*.

Ragnars saga lodbrókar ('The Saga of Ragnar Hairy-Breeks'). Describes the exploits of the great legendary hero. See *Fornaldarsögur*. Translated by M. Schlauch as *The Saga of the Volsung. The Saga of Ragnar Lodbrok . . .* (New York 1964).

Riddarasögur. A group of fictitious adventure tales, consisting of Norse translation of French romances on the one hand, and Icelandic imitations of them on the other. The boundary line between the *riddarasögur* and the *fornaldarsögur* is hard to define. Editions: Bjarni Vilhjálmsson, *Riddarasögur I–VI* (Reykjavik 1949–54); Agnete Loth, *Late Medieval Icelandic Romances I–V* (Copenhagen 1962–5).

A Glossary of Sagas and other Icelandic Texts

Rómverja saga ('The History of the Romans'). Consists of translations of extended portions from Sallust and Lucan. Dates from *c*.1200. Edited by K. Gislason in his *44 Pröver af oldnorsk Sprog og Litteratur* (Copenhagen 1860).

Seven Viking Romances. English translations by HP and PE of fictitious tales or *fornaldarsögur* (Penguin 1985).

Skjöldunga saga. The history of the legendary kings of Denmark, now lost apart from a fragment. See *IF XXXV* (Reykjavik 1987).

Snorra-Edda. See *Edda*.

Stjórn. A translation of certain parts of the Old Testament, including a good deal of exegetical matter. Edited by C.R. Unger (Christiania 1862).

Sturlaugs saga Starfsama. A fictitious adventure story involving witchcraft and heroic deeds. Translated by Otto Zitzelberger in his *The Two Versions of Sturlaugs Saga Starfsama: A Decipherment, Edition, and Translation of a Fourteenth-Century Icelandic Mythical-Heroic Saga* (Düsseldorf 1969).

Sturlunga saga. A collection of historical narratives dealing with events in Iceland during the period around 1117–1263. Edited by Jón Jóhannesson et al. (Reykjavik 1946); translated by Julia McCrew as *Sturlunga Saga I–II* (New York 1970 and 1975).

Styrbjarnar þáttur Sviakappa. Edited in *Flateyjarbók* (q.v.)

Sverris saga. A detailed factual account of the life of King Sverrir of Norway (d. 1202), composed by Abbot Karl Jónsson (d. 1212). Edited by Gustav Indrebø (Christiania 1920).

Þorláks saga biskups. Deals with the life and miracles of Iceland's national saint, St Thorlak, bishop of Skálholt (1178–93). Edited by Jón Helgason in *Byskupa Sögur 1, 2* (Copenhagen 1978); translated by Gudbrand Vigfusson and F. York Powell in *Origines Islandicae I* (Oxford 1905).

Þorvalds Þáttur hins viðförla ('The Story of Thorvald the Far-Traveller'). Edited by B. Kahle in *Altnordische Saga-Bibliothek XI* (Halle a.d.S. 1905); translated by Vigfusson and Powell as *The Tale of Thorvald the Far-Farer*', as above.

Trójumanna saga. Icelandic versions of the legend of Troy. Editions: Jonna Louis-Jensen, *Trójumanna saga* (Copenhagen 1963), and *Trójumanna saga. The Dares Phrygius Version* (Copenhagen 1981).

Veraldar saga ('The History of the World'). Based on learned Latin works, written *c*.1200. Edited by Jakob Benediktsson (Copenhagen 1944).

Vinland Sagas. A modern term for the two sagas describing the discovery of Vinland early in the eleventh century: *Eiriks saga rauda* and *Graelendinga saga*. Edited in *IF IV* (Reykjavik 1935); translated by MM and HP (Penguin 1965). See *Eiriks saga rauda*.

Ynglinga saga. See *Heimskringla*.

BIBLIOGRAPHY

1. Editions

The standard edition of *Yngvar's Saga* is Emil Olson's *Yngvars saga viðförla* (Copenhagen 1912). It is based on the two extant parchment MSS: AM 343, 4to in Arnamagnæan Collection in Reykjavik (-A), and GkS 2845, 4to in the Royal Library in Copenhagen (-B). There are also several papers MSS, of which Olson uses two: AM 343c, 4to (-C), and Rask/AM 2602, 4to (-D). The relationships between the MSS are discussed by Jón Helgason, 'Til Yngvars sagas overlevering', in *Opuscula* I. Bibliotheca Arnamagnæana 20 (Copenhagen 1960).

Manuscript B has appeared in a facsimile edition: *The Saga Manuscript 2845, 4to in the Old Royal Collection in the Royal Library of Copenhagen*. Manuscripta Islandica, vol. 2. Edited by Jón Helgason (Copenhagen 1955).

A popular edition, based on Olson's text is to be found in *Fornaldarsögur Norðurlanda* II (Reykjavik 1950).

Eymund's Saga is preserved in a single MS, viz. *Flateyjarbók*. See Glossary of Sagas and other Icelandic Texts.

2. Other works

N.T. Belaiew, 'Eymundar Saga and Icelandic Research in Russia,' *Saga-Book* II (1934).

Benedikt S. Benedikz and Sigfús Blöndal, *The Varangians of Byzantium* (Cambridge 1978).

N.K. Chadwick, *The Beginnings of Russian History* (Cambridge 1946).

Robert Cook, 'Russian History, Icelandic Story, and Byzantine Strategy in Eymundar Þáttr Hringssonar,' *Viator* 17 (1986). The most important work to date on *Eymund's Saga*.

Samuel Hazzard Cross, 'Yaroslav the Wise in Norse Tradition', *Speculum* 4 (1929).

H.R. Ellis Davidson, *The Viking Road to Byzantium* (London 1976).

Bibliography

Diotrich Hofmann, 'Die Yngvars saga víðförla und Oddr munkr inn fróði.', *Speculum norroenum*, edited by U. Dronke et al. (Odense 1981). A very important contribution.

'Zu Oddr Snorrasons Yngvars saga viðförla', *skandinavistik* 14 (1984).

Gwyn Jones, *A History of the Vikings* (Oxford 1968).

Mats G. Larsson, 'Yngvarr's Expedition and the *Georgian Chronicle*', in *Saga-Book* XXII (1987).

Kenneth H. Ober, 'O.I. Senkovskij, Russia's First Icelandic Scholar', *Scandinavian Studies* 40 (1968).

Omeljan Pritsak, *The Origin of Rus'*. *I. Old Scandinavian Sources other than the Sagas*. (Cambridge Mass 1981). Very important.

Alan C.S. Ross, *The Terfinnas and Beormas* (London 1981).

Peter H. Sawyer, *Kings and Vikings* (London 1982).

Jonathan Shepard, 'Yngvarr's Expedition to the East and a Russian Inscribed Stone Cross', *Saga-Book* XXI (1984-5). A major contribution; includes an excellent bibliography.

Sveriges runinskrifter I-XV (1900-81). In progress.

G. Turville-Petre, *Origins of Icelandic Literature* (Oxford 1953). A key work for the intellectual history of twelfth-century Iceland.

Dennis Ward, 'From the Varangians to the Greeks and other matters', Publications of the Modern Humanities Research Association, Vol. II: A Garland of Essays Offered to Professor Elizabeth Mary Hill; edited by R. Auby et al. (Cambridge 1970).

Elias Wissen, *Historiska runinskrifter* (1960).